Skills Worksheet

Directed Reading A

Section: A Solar System Is Born

1. Nine planets, the sun, and many moons and small bodies are part of our

_______________________.

THE SOLAR NEBULA

______ **2.** Nebulas are found in the regions of space
  a. outside the solar system.   **c.** inside stars.
  b. outside the force of gravity.   **d.** between stars.

______ **3.** Nebulas are mixtures of gases and
  a. water.   **c.** dust.
  b. vapor.   **d.** rock.

______ **4.** Which elements are mainly found in the gases of nebulas?
  a. hydrogen and helium   **c.** carbon dioxide and helium
  b. hydrogen and oxygen   **d.** carbon dioxide and oxygen

5. The matter of a nebula is held together by the force of

_______________________.

6. A measure of the average kinetic energy in an object is

_______________________.

7. How do gravity and pressure keep a nebula from collapsing?

____

____

____

UPSETTING THE BALANCE

8. What two events can upset the balance between gravity and pressure in a
nebula?

____

9. When a nebula collapses, small regions in the cloud called

_______________________ are pushed together.

10. The cloud of gas and dust that formed our solar system is called the

_______________________.

Directed Reading A *continued*

HOW THE SOLAR SYSTEM FORMED

_______**11.** As the solar nebula collapsed, the attraction between its particles
    a. decreased.   **c.** stayed the same.
    b. increased.   **d.** reversed.

_______**12.** The center of the collapsed cloud of gas and dust became
    a. very light and cool.   **c.** very dense and cool.
    b. very light and hot.   **d.** very dense and hot.

_______**13.** What happened to the solar nebula over time?
    a. It became cooler and lighter.
    b. It stopped rotating.
    c. It flattened into a rotating disk.
    d. It expanded into a large sphere.

14. In the solar nebula, bits of _________________ collided and stuck together to form small bodies.

15. The largest of the colliding bodies in the solar system are called

_________________, or small bodies.

16. Some of the largest planetesimals were far enough from the solar nebula to attract _________________.

17. Which planets are gas giants?

____

____

18. The inner planets of our solar system are made mostly of

_________________ material.

19. Which planets are inner planets?

____

____

20. After the planets formed, the center mass of the solar nebula became so

dense and hot that it formed _________________.

21. What happened when the gas in the nebula's center stopped collapsing?

____

____

Directed Reading A *continued*

Number the following events in the order in which they happened. Use the numbers –6. Write 1 for the first event that happened. Write 6 for the last event.

_______**22.** The largest planetesimals grew in size and attracted more gas and dust.

_______**23.** The solar nebula began to collapse.

_______**24.** The sun was born. The remaining gas and dust were removed from the solar system.

_______**25.** The solar nebula rotates and flattens. It grew warmer near its center.

_______**26.** Planets began to grow as planetesimals collided with one another.

_______**27.** Planetesimals began to form.

Directed Reading A

Section: The Sun: Our Very Own Star

_______ **1.** The sun is a large ball of gas made mostly of
  a. oxygen and carbon.
  b. hydrogen and helium.
  c. nitrogen and sulfur.
  d. carbon dioxide and oxygen.

THE STRUCTURE OF THE SUN

Match the correct description with the correct term. Write the letter in the space provided.

_______ **2.** the sun's outer atmosphere

_______ **3.** the thin region below the sun's corona

_______ **4.** the part of the sun that can be seen
    from Earth

_______ **5.** the region of the sun where gases circulate

_______ **6.** the center of the sun

_______ **7.** a very dense region of the sun

a. chromosphere

b. core

c. radiative zone

d. convective zone

e. corona

f. photosphere

ENERGY PRODUCTION IN THE SUN

_______ **8.** Early scientists thought that the sun produced its energy by
  a. rotating.
  b. expanding.
  c. collapsing inward.
  d. burning fuel.

_______ **9.** Scientists later thought that energy to heat the sun was released from
  a. gravity.   **c.** globules.
  b. pressure.   **d.** kinetic energy.

_______ **10.** Albert Einstein showed that matter and energy are
  a. the same.   **c.** unchanging.
  b. opposites.   **d.** interchangeable.

_______ **11.** What formula did Einstein use to show the relationship between
    matter and energy?
  a. $E = mc$ **c.** $M = ec$
  b. $E = mc^2$ **d.** $M = ec^2$

_______**12.** Einstein's formula states that energy equals mass times the
     a. speed of light.
     b. square of the speed of light.
     c. fusion of hydrogen.
     d. fusion of helium.

13. The process by which two or more low-mass nuclei combine to form another

nucleus is called ________________________.

14. What happens as four hydrogen nuclei fuse?

____

15. Energy is produced in the center, or ____________________, of the sun.

16. Energy passes from the sun's core through a dense region called the

________________________.

17. Hot gases are carried to the sun's visible surface from a region called the

________________________.

18. Energy leaves the sun as light from a region called the

________________________.

SOLAR ACTIVITY

_______**19.** The circulation of gases in the sun combines with the sun's rotation
     to create
     a. heat.
     b. radiation.
     c. electric fields.
     d. magnetic fields.

20. Why do some areas of the photosphere become cooler than surrounding areas?

____

____

____

____

21. Cooler, dark areas of the photosphere of the sun are called

________________________.

22. The sunspot cycle lasts about ____________________ years.

Directed Reading A *continued*

23. How might sunspot activity affect Earth?

____

____

____

24. Regions of very high temperature and brightness on the sun's surface are

called ___________________________.

25. How might Earth be affected by the eruption of solar flares?

____

____

____

Directed Reading A

Section: The Earth Takes Shape

______ **1.** What is Earth's position in the solar system?
   a. It is the closest planet to the sun.
   b. It is the farthest planet from the sun.
   c. It is the third planet from the sun.
   d. It is the seventh planet from the sun.

______ **2.** Earth is made mostly of
   a. rock.
   b. gases.
   c. marsh.
   d. volcanoes.

______ **3.** How much of Earth's surface is covered with water?
   a. one-half
   b. one-tenth
   c. three-fourths
   d. two-thirds

FORMATION OF THE SOLID EARTH

______ **4.** What bodies in the solar system combined to form Earth?
   a. nebulas
   b. stars
   c. asteroids
   d. planetesimals

______ **5.** What happened to Earth as gravity crushed the rock at its center?
   a. It formed an irregular shape.
   b. It became round.
   c. The moon formed.
   d. It rotated faster.

6. What two things helped Earth become warmer as it formed?

____

____

7. What caused the rocky material inside Earth to melt?

____

____

HOW THE EARTH'S LAYERS FORMED

8. As Earth's rocks melted, denser materials sank to Earth's center to form the

_______________________.

9. Less dense materials floated to Earth's surface to form the

_______________________.

10. The layer of earth beneath the crust is called the _______________________.

Match the correct description with the correct term. Write the letter in the space provided.

_______**11.** This is made up of materials such as magnesium and iron.

_______**12.** This is made up of nickel and iron.

_______**13.** This is made up of low density materials such as oxygen, silicon, and aluminum.

a. core

b. mantle

c. crust

FORMATION OF THE EARTH'S ATMOSPHERE

_______**14.** Most of Earth's atmosphere today is made up of
    a. carbon dioxide and helium.
    b. nitrogen and helium.
    c. carbon dioxide and oxygen.
    d. nitrogen and oxygen.

_______**15.** Scientists believe that Earth's early atmosphere was a mixture of carbon dioxide and
    a. water vapor.   **c.** oxygen.
    b. helium.   **d.** dust particles.

_______**16.** As Earth's early atmosphere changed, it probably formed from
    a. meteoroids.   **c.** crystal rock.
    b. hot springs.   **d.** volcanic gases.

_______**17.** As Earth's atmosphere changed, part of it may have come from icy planetesimals called
    a. moons.   **c.** ozones.
    b. comets.   **d.** glaciers.

Directed Reading A *continued*

18. Describe two factors that may have contributed to the formation of Earth's first oceans.

____

____

THE ROLE OF LIFE

19. Today, we are protected from the sun's ultraviolet rays by a layer of Earth's atmosphere called the _____________________.

20. Earth's early atmosphere probably did not have ozone, so many

_____________________ in the air and at the Earth's surface were broken apart.

21. The first _____________________ did not need oxygen and were protected by Earth's waters.

22. The process of absorbing energy from the sun and carbon dioxide from the air is called _____________________.

23. Early organisms released _____________________ during the process of making food.

24. As oxygen was added to the atmosphere, what gas was removed?

____

25. When did simple plants move onto land?

____

FORMATION OF OCEANS AND CONTINENTS

_______**26.** What factor probably caused the oceans to form?
- **a.** Materials in Earth's crust and mantle melted.
- **b.** Carbon dioxide in the atmosphere condensed into water.
- **c.** Oxygen from early organisms condensed into water.
- **d.** Earth cooled enough for rain to fall.

_______**27.** How long ago did a global ocean cover the planet?
- **a.** 4 billion years ago
- **b.** 40 million years ago
- **c.** 10 billion years ago
- **d.** 100 million years ago

Number the following events in the order in which they happened. Use the numbers 1–4. Write 1 for the first event that happened. Write 4 for the last event.

_______**28.** The earliest continents formed as lighter rocks rose to the surface of the earth.

_______**29.** The upper mantle cooled and became denser and heavier.

_______**30.** Thermal energy in the mantle caused continents to move.

_______**31.** Continents thickened and rose above the surface of the ocean.

Directed Reading A

Section: Planetary Motion
A REVOLUTION IN ASTRONOMY

1. How does Earth's rotation determine whether it is day or night?

____

____

____

Match the correct definition with the correct term. Write the letter in the space provided.

______ **2.** the spinning of a body on its axis

______ **3.** the path a body follows as it travels around another body in space

______ **4.** a complete trip along an orbit

______ **5.** the time it takes a planet to complete a single trip around the sun

a. revolution

b. rotation

c. period of revolution

d. orbit

6. According to Kepler's first law of motion, planets move in a(n)

_____________________ around the sun.

7. The maximum length of an ellipse, or a planet's orbit, is called its

_____________________.

8. A planet's maximum distance from the sun is the _________________ of its orbit.

9. According to Kepler's second law of motion, how does a planet's distance from the sun affect its motion?

____

____

____

Directed Reading A *continued*

10. According to Kepler's third law of motion, what information can be used to find a planet's distance from the sun?

____

____

NEWTON TO THE RESCUE!

_______**11.** What causes the planets that are closer to the sun to move faster?
 a. gravity
 b. heat
 c. magnetic fields
 d. solar energy

_______**12.** Newton discovered that the force of gravity depends on the distance between objects and the objects'
 a. volume.
 b. circumference.
 c. shape.
 d. mass.

_______**13.** The force of gravity between two objects increases if
 a. they have smaller masses and are farther apart.
 b. they have smaller masses and are closer together.
 c. they have larger masses and are farther apart.
 d. they have larger masses and are closer together.

_______**14.** An object's resistance in speed or direction is called
 a. mass.
 b. pressure.
 c. inertia.
 d. energy.

_______**15.** Gravity causes bodies in the solar system to
 a. repel one another.
 b. fall in a straight path.
 c. stay in orbit.
 d. move in a circular path.

Directed Reading B

Section: A Solar System Is Born

Circle the letter of the best answer for each question.

1. What do the planets of the solar system orbit around?

    a. many moons

    b. many stars

    c. the solar nebula

    d. the sun

THE SOLAR NEBULA

2. Where are nebulas in space?

    a. outside the solar system

    b. inside black holes

    c. inside stars

    d. between stars

3. What are nebulas made up of?

    a. gases and water

    b. energy and light

    c. gases and dust

    d. minerals and rock

4. What are the gases of a nebula made up of?

    a. hydrogen and helium

    b. hydrogen and oxygen

    c. carbon dioxide and helium

    d. carbon dioxide and oxygen

Directed Reading B *continued*

Gravity Pulls Matter Together
Circle the letter of the best answer for each question.

5. What are the gas and dust of a nebula made of?

a. solids

b. liquids

c. matter

d. air

6. What does gravity do to a nebula's matter?

a. It holds the matter together.

b. It pulls the matter apart.

c. It makes the matter drift away.

d. It makes the matter stronger.

Pressure Pushes Matter Apart
Read the words in the box. Read the sentences. Fill in each blank with the word or phrase that best completes the sentence.

solar nebula	globules
pressure	temperature

7. A measure of the energy of motion of the parts in an object is

_______________________.

8. A nebula is held together as gravity and

_______________________ balance each other.

UPSETTING THE BALANCE

9. Small gas clouds within a nebula are called

_______________________.

10. The cloud that made the solar system is called the

_______________________.

Directed Reading B *continued*

HOW THE SOLAR SYSTEM FORMED

Circle the letter of the best answer for each question.

11. What caused the solar system to form?

    a. Gravity became weaker.

    b. Pressure became weaker.

    c. The solar nebula collapsed.

    d. The solar nebula pulled together.

12. How did the solar nebula begin to move as it collapsed?

    a. side to side

    b. up and down

    c. in a cycle

    d. in a rotation

From Planetesimals to Planets

13. How did bits of dust in the nebula make planetesimals?

    a. They collided and stuck together.

    b. They became solid.

    c. They expanded from heat.

    d. They formed a sphere.

14. What are planetesimals?

    a. small nebulas

    b. small planets

    c. light gases

    d. new stars

| Directed Reading B *continued*

Gas Giant or Rocky Planet?

<u>Circle the letter</u> of the best answer for each question.

15. What type of planets are Jupiter, Saturn, Uranus, and Neptune?

    a. inner planets

    b. outer planets

    c. gas giants

    d. gas dwarves

16. What type of planets are Mercury, Venus, Earth, and Mars?

    a. inner planets

    b. outer planets

    c. gas giants

    d. gas dwarves

The Birth of A Star

17. What happened to the matter at the center of the nebula?

    a. It got cooler.

    b. It got lighter.

    c. It lost energy.

    d. It formed the sun.

18. At what point did the sun form?

    a. when the nebula exploded

    b. when gas left the nebula

    c. when gas stopped collapsing

    d. when helium atoms divided

Directed Reading B

Section: The Sun: Our Very Own Star

Circle the letter of the best answer for the question.

1. What is the sun mostly made of?

   a. iron and carbon

   b. oxygen and nitrogen

   c. hydrogen and helium

   d. sulfur and nickel

THE STRUCTURE OF THE SUN

Read the description. Then, draw a line from the dot next to each description to the matching word.

2. thin layer below the corona ●

3. part of the sun that we can see ● from Earth

4. forms the sun's outer ● atmosphere

    a. corona

    b. chromosphere

    c. photosphere

---

5. part of the sun where gases ● circulate

6. the center of the sun ●

7. a very dense part of the sun ●

    a. convective zone

    b. radiative zone

    c. core

ENERGY PRODUCTION IN THE SUN

Circle the letter of the best answer for each question.

8. How did early scientists think the sun made energy?

a. by making hydrogen

b. by storing gases

c. by burning dust

d. by burning fuel

Burning or Shrinking?

9. How did later scientists think the sun made energy?

a. from collapsing

b. from kinetic energy

c. from gravity

d. from pressure

Nuclear Fusion

10. What formula shows that matter can change into energy?

a. $C = {}^2em$

b. $E = mc^2$

c. $C = em$

d. $E = mc$

11. What is it called when small nuclei join to make another nucleus?

a. nuclear fusion

b. cellular fission

c. mitosis

d. combustion

Directed Reading B *continued*

Circle the letter of the best answer for the question.

12. What does nuclear fusion give the sun?

   a. volume

   b. mass

   c. brightness

   d. energy

Fusion in the Sun

Read the words in the box. Read the sentences. Fill in each blank with the word or phrase that best completes the sentence.

convective zone	core
radiative zone	photosphere

13. Energy is made in the _________________ of the sun.

14. The sun's energy moves from the core through the dense

_________________.

15. Hot gases carry energy from the _________________ to

the sun's surface.

16. Energy leaves the sun as light from the

_________________.

Circle the letter of the best answer for the question.

SOLAR ACTIVITY

17. What do the sun's energy and rotation create?

   a. solar eclipses

   b. change of seasons

   c. high temperatures

   d. magnetic fields

Sunspots

Circle the letter of the best answer for each question.

18. What part of the sun can have sunspots?

    a. the core   **c.** the corona

    b. the photosphere   **d.** the chromosphere

19. What are sunspots?

    a. cool, dark spots

    b. hot, bright spots

    c. spots with weak magnetic fields

    d. spots that carry energy

Climate Confusion

20. How might sunspots affect Earth?

    a. They might cause lightning.

    b. They might cause erosion.

    c. They might affect temperatures.

    d. They might affect photosynthesis.

Solar Flares

21. What are very hot and bright regions on the sun's surface?

    a. sunspots

    b. solar flares

    c. supernovas

    d. black holes

22. What can solar flares interrupt on Earth?

    a. electricity

    b. weather

    c. radio communications

    d. telephone lines

Directed Reading B

Section: The Earth Takes Shape

Circle the letter of the best answer for each question.

1. What is Earth mostly made of?

   a. rock

   b. grass

   c. dust

   d. gas

2. What is the Earth's surface mostly covered with?

   a. water

   b. gas

   c. dust

   d. grass

FORMATION OF THE SOLID EARTH

3. What did planetesimals do as Earth formed?

   a. collapsed inward

   b. traveled around the sun

   c. left the solar system

   d. crashed and combined

The Effects of Gravity

4. What happened to Earth as gravity crushed rock at its center?

   a. It became flat.

   b. It became round.

   c. It got cooler.

   d. It started spinning.

| Directed Reading B *continued*

The Effects of Heat
Circle the letter of the best answer for each question.

5. What heated Earth as it formed?

   a. solar flares

   b. radioactive material

   c. sunspots

   d. volcanoes

6. What happened as Earth heated up?

   a. The oceans dried up.

   b. Fire covered Earth.

   c. Inner rocks melted.

   d. Forms of life grew.

HOW THE EARTH'S LAYERS FORMED
Read the description. Then, draw a line from the dot next to each description to the matching word.

7. thin, outermost layer of Earth ●   **a.** crust

8. central part of Earth ●   **b.** mantle

9. layer beneath the crust ●   **c.** core

FORMATION OF THE EARTH'S ATMOSPHERE
Circle the letter of the best answer for the question.

10. What makes up most of Earth's atmosphere today?

   a. nitrogen and oxygen

   b. hydrogen and helium

   c. sulfur and chlorine

   d. iron and nickel

Directed Reading B *continued*

Earth's First Atmosphere
Circle the letter of the best answer for each question.

11. What might have made up Earth's early atmosphere?

    a. sulfur and steam

    b. nitrogen and dust

    c. oxygen and water vapor

    d. carbon dioxide and water vapor

Earth's Second Atmosphere

12. What probably changed Earth's early atmosphere?

    a. meteoroids

    b. hot springs

    c. crystal rock

    d. volcanic gases

13. What might have helped change part of the early atmosphere?

    a. gases in moons

    b. elements in comets

    c. energy in ozones

    d. water in springs

14. How might water vapor have formed the first oceans?

    a. It froze.

    b. It melted.

    c. It condensed.

    d. It evaporated.

15. What might have brought some water to the first oceans?

    a. meteor showers

    b. heavy snowfall

    c. icy comets

    d. hot springs

| Directed Reading B *continued*

THE ROLE OF LIFE
Ultraviolet Radiation
Read the description. Then, <u>draw a line</u> from the dot next to each description to the matching word.

16. has a lot of energy and can break ● apart molecules

a. ozone layer

17. protects us from the rays of ● the sun

b. life-forms

c. ultraviolet radiation

18. may have started forming from ● molecules in Earth's waters

The Source of Oxygen

19. a way organisms make food by ● using the sun's energy

a. oxygen

20. a gas that is added to air as ● organisms make food

b. photosynthesis

c. carbon dioxide

21. a gas that is removed from air as ● organisms make food

FORMATION OF OCEANS AND CONTINENTS
<u>Circle the letter</u> of the best answer for the question.

22. What caused a global ocean to form when Earth cooled?

    a. snow

    b. rain

    c. steam

    d. glaciers

Directed Reading B *continued*

Circle the letter of the best answer for each question.

23. What are the continents of Earth made up of?

  a. rock

  b. water

  c. gases

  d. algae

The Growth of Continents

24. What happened as light rocks piled on Earth's surface?

  a. Mountains formed.

  b. The oceans got smaller.

  c. The mantle got lighter.

  d. Early continents formed.

25. What made the early continents move around?

  a. energy in the mantle

  b. hot springs in the mantle

  c. heavy earthquakes

  d. melting ice

Directed Reading B

Section: Planetary Motion

A REVOLUTION IN ASTRONOMY

Read the description. Then, <u>draw a line</u> from the dot next to each description to the matching word.

1. the time a planet takes to finish one trip around the sun ●

2. the spinning of a planet on its axis ●

3. one complete trip around the sun ●

4. the path a planet follows when it travels around the sun ●

a. orbit

b. rotation

c. period of revolution

d. revolution

Kepler's First Law of Motion

<u>Circle the letter</u> of the best answer for each question.

5. What shape do planets follow when they travel around the sun?

a. a parallelogram

b. an ellipse

c. a diamond

d. a rhombus

Kepler's Second Law of Motion

6. How does a planet move if it is closer to the sun?

a. smoother

b. rougher

c. slower

d. faster

Directed Reading B *continued*

Kepler's Third Law of Motion

Circle the letter of the best answer for each question.

7. What can be used to find a planet's distance from the sun?

   a. the planet's mass

   b. the planet's size

   c. the planet's period of revolution

   d. the planet's number of moons

NEWTON TO THE RESCUE!

8. What makes some planets move faster around the sun?

   a. heat

   b. energy

   c. pressure

   d. gravity

The Law of Universal Gravitation

9. What happens to the force of gravity if objects have more mass?

   a. It increases.

   b. It decreases.

   c. It stays the same.

   d. It is broken.

10. What happens to the force of gravity if objects move farther apart?

   a. It increases.   **c.** It stays the same.

   b. It decreases.   **d.** It is broken.

Orbits Falling Down and Around

11. What does gravity make planets do?

   a. stay in orbit   **c.** pull away from each other

   b. move in a circle   **d.** crash into each other

Vocabulary and Section Summary

A Solar System Is Born

VOCABULARY

In your own words, write a definition of the following terms in the space provided.

1. nebula

____

____

2. solar nebula

____

____

SECTION SUMMARY

Read the following section summary.

- The solar system formed out of a vast cloud of gas and dust called the *nebula*.
- Gravity and pressure were balanced, until something upset the balance. Then the nebula began to collapse.
- Collapse of the solar nebula caused heating at the center, while planetesimals formed in surrounding space.
- The central mass of the nebula became the sun. Planets formed from the surrounding materials.

Vocabulary and Section Summary

The Sun: Our Very Own Star

VOCABULARY

In your own words, write a definition of the following terms in the space provided.

1. nuclear fusion

____

____

2. sunspot

____

____

SECTION SUMMARY

Read the following section summary.

- The sun is a large ball of gas made mostly of hydrogen and helium. The sun consists of many layers.
- The sun's energy comes from nuclear fusion that takes place in the center of the sun.
- The visible surface of the sun, or the photosphere, is very active.
- Sunspots and solar flares are the result of the sun's magnetic fields that reach space.
- Sunspot activity may affect Earth's climate, and solar flares can interact with Earth's atmosphere.

Skills Worksheet

Vocabulary and Section Summary

The Earth Takes Shape

VOCABULARY

In your own words, write a definition of the following terms in the space provided.

1. crust

____

____

2. mantle

____

____

3. core

____

____

SECTION SUMMARY

Read the following section summary.

- The effects of gravity and heat created the shape and structure of Earth.
- The Earth is divided into three main layers based on composition: the crust, mantle, and core.
- The presence of life dramatically changed Earth's atmosphere by adding free oxygen.
- Earth's oceans formed shortly after the Earth did, when it had cooled off enough for rain to fall. Continents formed when lighter materials gathered on the surface and rose above sea level.

Vocabulary and Section Summary

Planetary Motion

VOCABULARY

In your own words, write a definition of the following terms in the space provided.

1. rotation

2. orbit

3. revolution

SECTION SUMMARY

Read the following section summary.

- Rotation is the spinning of a planet on its axis, and revolution is one complete trip along an orbit.
- Planets move in an ellipse around the sun. The closer they are to the sun, the faster they move. The period of a planet's revolution depends on the planet's semimajor axis.
- Gravitational attraction decreases as distance increases and as mass decreases.

Section Review

A Solar System Is Born

USING KEY TERMS

1. In your own words, write a definition for each of the following terms: *nebula* and *solar nebula.*

____

____

UNDERSTANDING KEY IDEAS

_______ **2.** What is the relationship between gravity and pressure in a nebula?
    a. Gravity reduces pressure.
    b. Pressure balances gravity.
    c. Pressure increases gravity.
    d. None of the above

3. Describe how our solar system formed.

____

____

____

____

4. Compare the inner planets with the outer planets.

____

____

____

____

Section Review *continued*

MATH SKILLS

5. If the planets, moons, and other bodies make up 0.15% of the solar system's mass, what percentage does the sun make up? Show your work below.

CRITICAL THINKING

6. Evaluating Hypotheses Pluto, the outermost planet, is small and rocky. Some scientists argue that Pluto is a captured asteroid, not a planet. Use what you know about how solar systems form to evaluate this hypothesis.

____

____

____

7. Making Inferences Why do all of the planets go around the sun in the same direction, and why do the planets lie on a relatively flat plane?

____

____

____

Section Review

The Sun: Our Very Own Star

USING KEY TERMS

1. In your own words, write a definition for each of the following terms: *sunspot* and *nuclear fusion*.

____

____

UNDERSTANDING KEY IDEAS

______ **2.** Which of the following statements describes how energy is produced in the sun?

    a. The sun burns fuels to generate energy.

    b. As hydrogen changes into helium deep inside the sun, a great deal of energy is made.

    c. Energy is released as the sun shrinks because of gravity.

    d. None of the above

3. Describe the composition of the sun.

____

____

4. Name and describe the layers of the sun.

____

____

____

5. In which area of the sun do sunspots appear?

____

____

____

6. Explain how sunspots form.

____

____

____

Section Review *continued*

7. Describe how sunspots can affect the Earth.

____

____

8. What are solar flares, and how do they form?

____

____

____

MATH SKILLS

9. If the equatorial diameter of the sun is 1.39 million km, how many kilometers is the sun's radius? Show your work below.

CRITICAL THINKING

10. Applying Concepts If nuclear fusion in the sun's core suddenly stopped today, would the sky be dark in the daytime tomorrow? Explain.

____

____

____

11. Making Comparisons Compare the theories that scientists proposed about the source of the sun's energy with the process of nuclear fusion in the sun.

____

____

____

Section Review

The Earth Takes Shape

USING KEY TERMS

1. Use each of the following terms in a separate sentence: *crust, mantle,* and *core.*

____

____

____

UNDERSTANDING KEY IDEAS

______ **2.** Earth's first atmosphere was mostly made of
   a. nitrogen and oxygen.
   b. chlorine, nitrogen, and sulfur.
   c. carbon dioxide and water vapor.
   d. water vapor and oxygen.

3. Describe the structure of the Earth.

____

____

____

4. Why did the Earth separate into distinct layers?

____

____

____

5. Describe the development of Earth's atmosphere. How did life affect Earth's atmosphere?

____

____

____

____

Section Review *continued*

6. Explain how Earth's oceans and continents formed.

____

____

CRITICAL THINKING

7. Applying Concepts How did the effects of gravity help shape the Earth?

____

____

____

8. Making Inferences How would the removal of forests affect the Earth's atmosphere?

____

____

____

INTERPRETING GRAPHICS

Use the illustration below to answer the questions that follow.

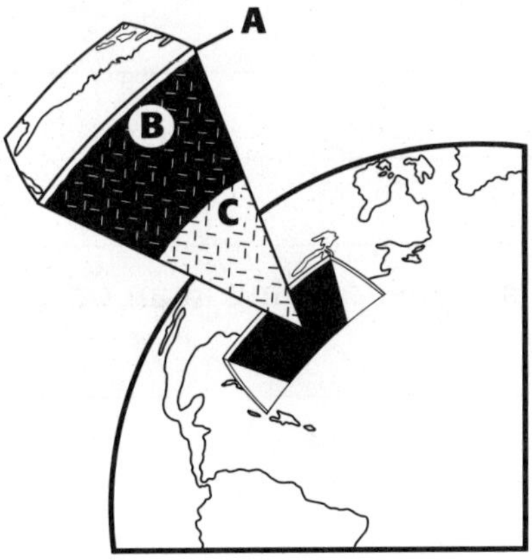

9. Which of the layers is composed mostly of the elements magnesium and iron?

____

10. Which of the layers is composed mostly of the elements iron and nickel?

____

Section Review

Planetary Motion

USING KEY TERMS

1. In your own words, write a definition for each of the following terms: *revolution* and *rotation*.

____

____

____

____

UNDERSTANDING KEY IDEAS

______ **2.** Kepler discovered that planets move faster when they
  a. are farther from the sun.
  b. are closer to the sun.
  c. have more mass.
  d. rotate faster.

3. On what properties does the force of gravity between two objects depend?

____

____

____

4. How does gravity keep a planet moving in an orbit around the sun?

____

____

____

____

| Section Review *continued*

MATH SKILLS

5. The Earth's period of revolution is 365.25 days. Convert this period of revolution into hours. Show your work below.

CRITICAL THINKING

6. Applying Concepts If a planet had two moons and one moon was twice as far from the planet as the other, which moon would complete a revolution of the planet first? Explain your answer.

____

____

____

____

____

____

7. Making Comparisons Describe the three laws of planetary motion. How is each law related to the other laws?

____

____

____

____

____

____

____

Chapter Review

USING KEY TERMS

Complete each of the following sentences by choosing the correct term from the word bank.

nebula	crust
mantle	solar nebula

1. A _________________________ is a large cloud of gas and dust in interstellar space.

2. The _________________________ lies between the core and the crust of the Earth.

For each pair of terms, explain how the meanings of the terms differ.

3. *nebula* and *solar nebula*

____

____

4. *crust* and *mantle*

____

____

5. *rotation* and *revolution*

____

____

6. *nuclear fusion* and *sunspot*

____

____

UNDERSTANDING KEY IDEAS

Multiple Choice

_______ 7. To determine a planet's period of revolution, you must know its
  a. size.
  b. mass.
  c. orbit.
  d. All of the above

Chapter Review *continued*

_______ **8.** During Earth's formation, materials such as nickel and iron sank to the
    a. mantle.   **c.** crust.
    b. core.   **d.** All of the above

_______ **9.** Planetary orbits are shaped like
    a. orbits.
    b. spirals.
    c. ellipses.
    d. periods of revolution.

_______ **10.** Impacts in the early solar system
    a. brought new materials to the planets.
    b. released energy.
    c. dug craters.
    d. All of the above

_______ **11.** Organisms that photosynthesize get their energy from
    a. nitrogen.   **c.** the sun.
    b. oxygen.   **d.** water.

_______ **12.** Which of the following planets has the shortest period of revolution?
    a. Pluto   **c.** Mercury
    b. Earth   **d.** Jupiter

_______ **13.** Which gas in Earth's atmosphere suggests that there is life on Earth?
    a. hydrogen   **c.** carbon dioxide
    b. oxygen   **d.** nitrogen

_______ **14.** Which layer of the Earth has the lowest density?
    a. the core   **c.** the crust
    b. the mantle   **d.** None of the above

_______ **15.** What is the measure of the average kinetic energy of particles in an
object?
    a. temperature   **c.** gravity
    b. pressure   **d.** force

Short Answer

16. Compare a sunspot with a solar flare.

____

____

17. Describe how the Earth's oceans and continents formed.

____

____

Chapter Review *continued*

18. Explain how pressure and gravity may have become unbalanced in the solar nebula.

____

____

19. Define *nuclear fusion* in your own words. Describe how nuclear fusion generates the sun's energy.

____

____

CRITICAL THINKING

20. Concept Mapping Use the following terms to create a concept map: *solar nebula, solar system, planetesimals, sun, photosphere, core, nuclear fusion, planets,* and *Earth.*

Chapter Review *continued*

21. Making Comparisons How did Newton's law of universal gravitation help explain the work of Johannes Kepler?

____

____

____

22. Predicting Consequences Using what you know about the relationship between living things and the development of Earth's atmosphere, explain how the formation of ozone holes in Earth's atmosphere could affect living things.

____

____

23. Identifying Relationships Describe Kepler's three laws of motion in your own words. Describe how each law relates to either the revolution, rotation, or orbit of a planetary body.

____

____

____

INTERPRETING GRAPHICS

Use the illustration below to answer the questions that follow.

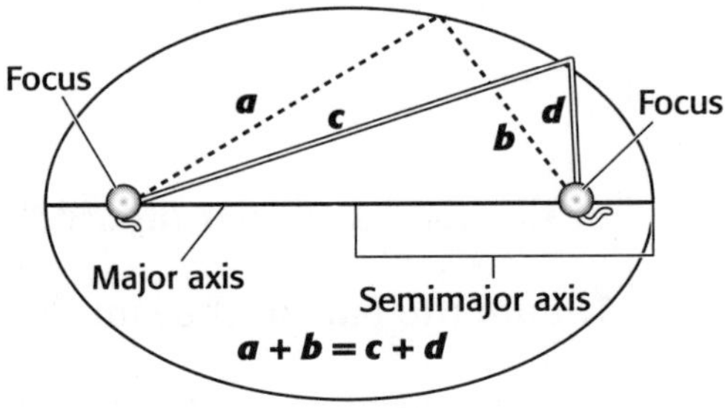

24. Which of Kepler's laws of motion does the illustration represent?

____

25. How does the equation shown above support the law?

____

____

26. What is an ellipse's maximum length called?

____

Reinforcement

Stay on the Sunny Side

Complete this worksheet after you finish reading the section, "The Sun: Our Very Own Star." Write one of these terms in the corresponding layer of the diagram of the sun: *chromosphere, photosphere, radiative zone, core, corona,* **or** *convective zone.*

Use the names of the layers of the sun to answer the riddles.

_______________________ **1.** I am the part of the sun that you can see.

_______________________ **2.** I am a very dense layer of the sun that blocks energy.

_______________________ **3.** I am the sun's outer atmosphere.

_______________________ **4.** I am the thin layer below the corona.

_______________________ **5.** I am the layer of the sun where energy is made.

_______________________ **6.** I am the layer of the sun where gases circulate.

Reinforcement

Third Rock from the Sun

Complete this worksheet after you finish reading the section "The Earth Takes Shape."

1. Complete the timeline about the development of Earth. Write each event listed below next to the correct time period.

Events

- Simple plants move onto land.
- The upper mantle becomes heavier.
- Continents start to grow.
- A global ocean covers Earth.
- Earth forms.
- Organisms carry out photosynthesis.

4.6 billion years ago ____

4 billion years ago ____

3.4 billion years ago ____

2.5 billion years ago ____

2.2 billion years ago ____

1.5 billion years ago ____

2. How did the presence of organisms play a role in changing Earth's atmosphere?

____

____

____

____

____

____

Critical Thinking

A Balooney Solar System

Walter P. Balooney came up with a new theory about the formation of the solar system. Read and analyze his ideas below.

Life cannot possibly exist in any solar system other than our own. Therefore, our solar system must have developed differently from all the others in space. I think the government is wasting our hard-earned tax dollars by funding searches for other solar systems and nebulae in deep space. Not only does my theory make perfect sense, it also requires little or no tax money for research.

Billions of years ago, our nine planets were floating through space, each moving in a different direction. The first planet to come near the sun was Mercury. As it began traveling around the sun, the force of gravity was created. This new force began pulling the other eight planets from the far reaches of deep space and into orbit around our sun. When the last planet, Pluto, fell into orbit, the solar system was completed.

USEFUL TERMS

assumption something that is believed to be true without proof or evidence

RECOGNIZING FALLACIES

1. Walter P. Balooney believes our solar system formed differently from others in space. Does he present a logical explanation for his idea? Explain your answer.

____

____

____

____

2. Does Mr. Balooney's theory rely on any unproven assumptions? Explain your answer.

____

____

____

____

Critical Thinking *continued*

FORMING AN OPINION

3. Does Mr. Balooney's argument show any bias? Explain your answer.

____

____

____

____

DETERMINING CAUSE AND EFFECT

4. Where in his theory does Mr. Balooney confuse cause and effect?

____

____

____

____

UNDERSTANDING CONCEPTS

5. Mr. Balooney claims that the sun's gravity pulled planets from the far reaches of space and into their present orbits. What is wrong with this idea?

____

____

____

____

DEMONSTRATING REASONED JUDGMENT

6. Name one important characteristic of solar system formation that Mr. Balooney's theory does not explain.

____

____

____

Section Quiz

Section: A Solar System Is Born

Match the correct description with the correct term. Write the letter in the space provided.

_______ **1.** the force that holds together the matter of a nebula

_______ **2.** the force created as particles in a nebula push away from each other

_______ **3.** large bodies that became the cores of current planets

_______ **4.** the cloud of gas and dust that formed our solar system

_______ **5.** a large cloud of gas and dust in interstellar space

_______ **6.** a measure of the energy of motion of the particles in an object

a. nebula

b. solar nebula

c. temperature

d. pressure

e. gravity

f. planetesimals

Write the letter of the correct answer in the space provided.

_______ **7.** A nebula is held together by the balance of
  a. the outward force of gravity and inward pressure.
  b. the inward force of gravity and outward pressure.
  c. high and low kinetic energies.
  d. high and low temperatures.

_______ **8.** After the solar nebula collapsed, its center became very hot and
  a. more nebulas formed.
  b. it formed into a sphere.
  c. planetesimals formed.
  d. it exploded.

_______ **9.** Planets began to form as
  a. planetesimals collided and combined.
  b. planetesimals flattened into rotating disks.
  c. temperatures in the solar nebula fell.
  d. gravity held together the solar nebula.

_______ **10.** The extra matter at the center of the solar nebula became the
  a. inner planets.   **c.** sun.
  b. moon.   **d.** super nova.

Section Quiz

Section: The Sun: Our Very Own Star

Match the correct description with the correct term. Write the letter in the space provided.

_______ **1.** giant eruptions on the sun's surface

_______ **2.** caused by the rotation and movement of energy of the sun, and reach far out into space

_______ **3.** the visible surface of the sun

_______ **4.** a dense layer of the sun where light and energy are blocked and sent into different directions

_______ **5.** when two or more nuclei fuse to form another nucleus; the source of the sun's energy

_______ **6.** may be affected on Earth by the surface activity of the sun

_______ **7.** cooler, dark areas of the photosphere of the sun

_______ **8.** the layer of the sun where gases circulate and carry energy to the visible surface of the sun

_______ **9.** the outermost layer of the sun

_______ **10.** where the suns' energy is made; the innermost layer of the sun

a. nuclear fusion

b. sunspots

c. solar flares

d. core

e. corona

f. radiative zone

g. convective zone

h. photosphere

i. climate

j. magnetic fields

Section Quiz

Section: The Earth Takes Shape

Write the letter of the correct answer in the space provided.

_______ **1.** What bodies in the solar system collided and combined to form Earth?
- **a.** globules
- **b.** stars
- **c.** craters
- **d.** planetesimals

_______ **2.** What factors caused the shape and structure of Earth?
- **a.** gravity and energy
- **b.** heat and pressure
- **c.** gravity and heat
- **d.** energy and pressure

_______ **3.** Earth's layers formed as rocks melted and
- **a.** heavier and lighter elements separated.
- **b.** lava from volcanoes covered Earth.
- **c.** different landforms developed.
- **d.** earthquakes caused elements to settle.

_______ **4.** The layer of Earth that extends to the planet's center is the
- **a.** crust.
- **b.** corona.
- **c.** mantle.
- **d.** core.

_______ **5.** The middle layer of Earth is the
- **a.** crust.
- **b.** meridian.
- **c.** mantle.
- **d.** core.

_______ **6.** The layer of Earth that has the lightest elements is the
- **a.** mantle.
- **b.** core.
- **c.** crust.
- **d.** ozone.

_______ **7.** Early life-forms released oxygen into Earth's atmosphere through the process of
- **a.** photosynthesis.
- **b.** osmosis.
- **c.** oxidation.
- **d.** pollination.

_______ **8.** Scientists think that Earth's first atmosphere was made up of
- **a.** oxygen and water vapor.
- **b.** carbon dioxide and water vapor.
- **c.** volcanic gases and dust.
- **d.** hydrogen and cirrus clouds

_______ **9.** Scientists think oceans may have formed after millions of years of
- **a.** evaporation
- **b.** rainfall.
- **c.** flooding.
- **d.** humidity.

Name _______________________________ Class _______________ Date ____________

Section Quiz

Section: Planetary Motion

Match the correct definition with the correct term. Write the letter in the space provided.

_______ 1. one complete trip along an orbit

_______ 2. the path of a body that travels around another body in space

_______ 3. the amount of time it takes a body to complete a trip along an orbit

_______ 4. the spin of a body on its axis

a. rotation

b. orbit

c. revolution

d. period of revolution

Write the letter of the correct answer in the space provided.

_______ 5. Each planet moves around in the sun in
   a. a path the shape of a circle.   **c.** a path the shape of a spiral.
   b. a path the shape of an ellipse.   **d.** similar-sized orbits.

_______ 6. The closer a planet is to the sun,
   a. the slower it travels around the sun.
   b. the faster it travels around the sun.
   c. the smaller the angle of its axis.
   d. the greater the angle of its axis.

_______ 7. The period of a planet's revolution can be used to calculate the planet's
   a. total mass.   **c.** distance from the sun.
   b. total circumference.   **d.** diameter to the sun.

_______ 8. The gravitational attraction between two objects increases if
   a. their volumes increase.
   b. their volumes decrease.
   c. the distance between them increases.
   d. the distance between them decreases.

_______ 9. The gravitational attraction between two objects decreases if
   a. their masses decrease.
   b. their masses increase.
   c. their total area decreases.
   d. their total area increases.

_______ 10. What is an object's resistance in speed or direction?
   a. gravity   **c.** pressure
   b. kinetic energy   **d.** inertia

Chapter Test A

Formation of the Solar System
MATCHING

Match the correct description with the correct term. Write the letter in the space provided.

_______ **1.** the visible layer of the sun

_______ **2.** a complete trip along an orbit

_______ **3.** the process that provides the sun with its energy

_______ **4.** the layer of Earth that formed as lighter elements floated to the surface

_______ **5.** the spinning of a body on its axis

_______ **6.** the layer of Earth above the core

_______ **7.** a huge eruption on the surface of the sun

_______ **8.** a cooler, dark area of the photosphere

_______ **9.** the path a body follows as it travels around another body in space

_______ **10.** a cloud of gas and dust from which bodies in space are formed

a. sunspot

b. revolution

c. rotation

d. orbit

e. mantle

f. nebula

g. nuclear fusion

h. crust

i. photosphere

j. solar flare

| Chapter Test A *continued*

MULTIPLE CHOICE

Write the letter of the correct answer in the space provided.

_______11. What caused the solar system to form?
   a. the birth of a nearby star
   b. the collapse of the solar nebula
   c. nuclear fusion in the sun
   d. the growth of the solar nebula

_______12. What two factors affect the gravitational attraction between
   two objects?
   a. surface area and mass
   b. distance and circumference
   c. volume and mass
   d. distance and mass

_______13. Early organisms added oxygen to Earth's atmosphere as they made
   food through
   a. photosynthesis.
   b. fission.
   c. germination.
   d. oxidation.

_______14. Earth's period of revolution is about
   a. one day.
   b. one week.
   c. one year.
   d. three months.

_______15. What two opposing forces must stay balanced to keep a nebula
   from collapsing?
   a. gravity and temperature
   b. inertia and pressure
   c. gravity and pressure
   d. temperature and inertia

_______16. Earth's early continents formed as rocks melted and
   a. absorbed much of the water covering the planet.
   b. lighter materials rose above the ocean's surface.
   c. the heaviest materials rose to form the planet's crust.
   d. sank below the ocean's surface.

Holt Science and Technology   **53**   Formation of the Solar System

MULTIPLE CHOICE

Write the letter of the correct answer in the space provided.

_______ **17.** What may have caused oceans to form during Earth's second atmosphere?
    a. The Earth had cooled enough for heavy rain to fall.
    b. Nitrogen gases condensed into water.
    c. The moon released icy dust particles that crashed into Earth.
    d. Millions of years of meteor showers fell upon Earth.

_______ **18.** The planets of the solar system formed as
    a. the center of the gas cloud cooled.
    b. planetesimals flattened into a rotating disk.
    c. planetesimals collided into one another.
    d. the sun absorbed extra gas and dust from the solar system.

_______ **19.** In what layer of the sun is energy produced?
    a. photosphere
    b. convective zone
    c. chromosphere
    d. core

_______ **20.** What factor allowed the sun to form in the solar system?
    a. the explosion of planetesimals
    b. the division of hydrogen atoms
    c. intense heat at the center of the solar nebula
    d. the division of helium atoms

_______ **21.** How might Earth be affected by the activity of sunspots on the sun's surface?
    a. Sunspot activity might affect Earth's temperatures.
    b. Low sunspot activity might contribute to global warming.
    c. Sunspot activity could send electrically charged particles into Earth's atmosphere.
    d. Sunspot activity has been linked to hurricanes.

_______ **22.** What happens during nuclear fusion in the sun?
    a. Oxygen nuclei combine to form helium.
    b. Helium nuclei combine to form oxygen.
    c. Helium nuclei combine to form hydrogen.
    d. Hydrogen nuclei combine to form helium.

Chapter Test A *continued*

MULTIPLE CHOICE

Use the figure below to answer questions 23–25. Write the letter of the correct answer in the space provided.

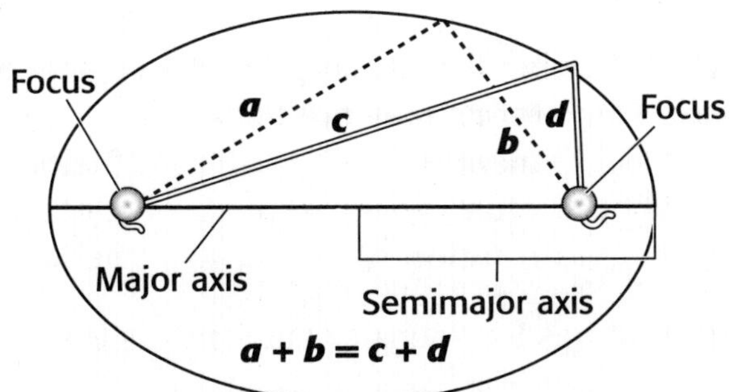

_______**23.** The shape of the ellipse above describes
    a. the cross section of the sun.
    b. the shape of a planet's core.
    c. the path of a planet's axis.
    d. a planet's orbit around the sun.

_______**24.** The length of the semimajor axis can be used to describe
    a. the surface area of the sun.
    b. the radius of the sun.
    c. the distance between a planet and the sun.
    d. the radius of a planet's orbit around the sun.

_______**25.** The longer the length of the semimajor axis,
    a. the longer it takes a planet to orbit the sun.
    b. the longer it takes energy to leave the sun.
    c. the faster a planet can spin on its axis.
    d. the heavier the mass of a planet.

Chapter Test B

Formation of the Solar System

USING KEY TERMS

Use the terms from the following list to complete the sentences below. Each term may be used only once. Some terms may not be used.

sunspot	mantle	fusion
solar flare	crust	globule
revolution	rotation	nebula

1. The layer of Earth that has low-density materials is the

_______________________.

2. A large, interstellar cloud of gas and dust is called a

_______________________.

3. The sun is powered by nuclear _______________________.

4. A cooler area of the photosphere that may affect climate on Earth is a

_______________________.

5. Earth completes one _______________________ each day.

UNDERSTANDING KEY IDEAS

Write the letter of the correct answer in the space provided.

_______ **6.** In a young solar system, new materials are added to planets by
- **a.** nuclear fusion.
- **b.** primitive life-forms.
- **c.** the collisions of smaller bodies.
- **d.** convection in planet layers.

_______ **7.** Much of the water of the early oceans may have been
- **a.** condensed from volcanic gases.
- **b.** created by the reaction of hydrogen gas and iron.
- **c.** created by the interaction of UV light and oxygen.
- **d.** absorbed by Earth's core.

_______ **8.** A planet with a large orbit has a
- **a.** slow rotation.
- **b.** large gas ring.
- **c.** long period of revolution.
- **d.** large surface area.

_______ **9.** The dense layer of the sun that blocks light and energy is the
- **a.** convective zone.
- **b.** radiative zone.
- **c.** photosphere.
- **d.** chromosphere.

Chapter Test B *continued*

_______**10.** The gravitational attraction between two objects increases if
   a. the distance between them increases and their mass increases.
   b. the distance between them decreases and their mass decreases.
   c. the distance between them increases and their mass decreases.
   d. the distance between them decreases and their mass increases.

11. Briefly state Kepler's three laws of planetary motion.

____

____

____

____

12. How did the interior of Earth separate into layers?

____

____

____

13. How do gravity and pressure keep a nebula from collapsing?

____

____

____

CRITICAL THINKING

14. Why do the planets of the solar system have different qualities even though they came from the same nebula?

____

____

____

____

15. Why are the planets in the solar system shaped like spheres?

____

____

____

____

____

16. How might Earth's atmosphere be affected if large areas of forest are lost?

____

____

____

____

INTERPRETING GRAPHICS

Use the graph below to answer question 17.

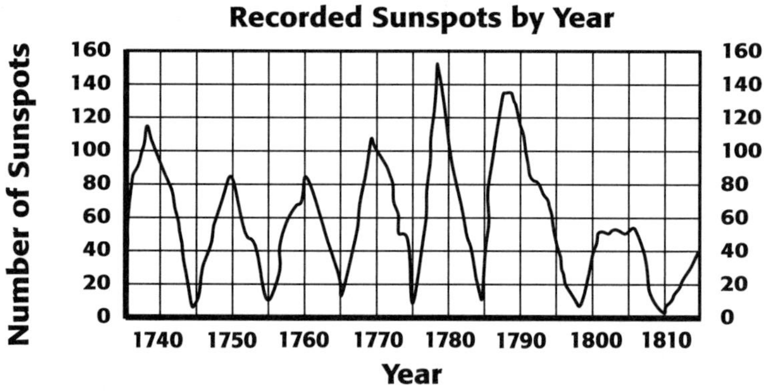

Recorded Sunspots by Year

17. The graph shows the number of sunspots recorded each year from 1735 to 1815. About how much time passed between the year with the most sunspots and the year with the fewest sunspots? Explain your answer.

____

____

____

____

| Chapter Test B *continued*

CONCEPT MAPPING

18. Use the following terms to complete the concept map below:

planetesimals	gas	nebula
planets	solar system	gravity
solar nebula	rock	

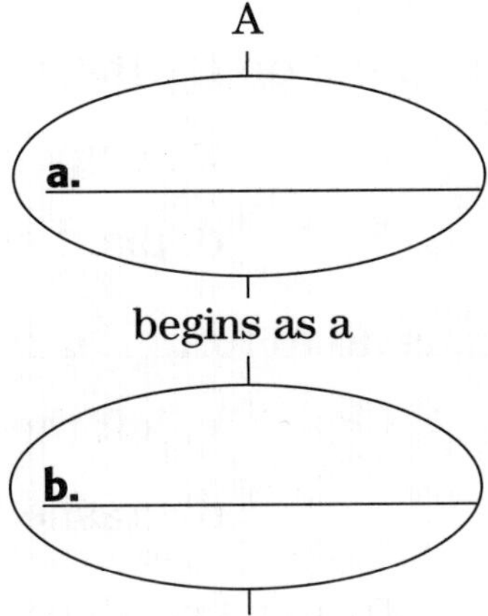

A

a. _______________

begins as a

b. _______________

which is pulled together by

c. _______________

to form a

d. _______________

where bits of dust and rock form

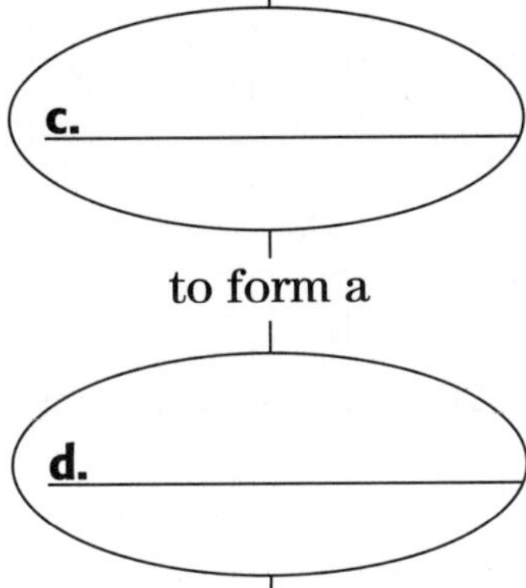

e. _______________

which develop into

f. _______________

which are made mostly of

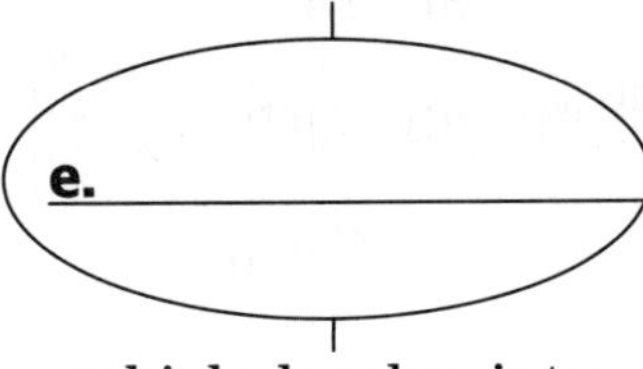

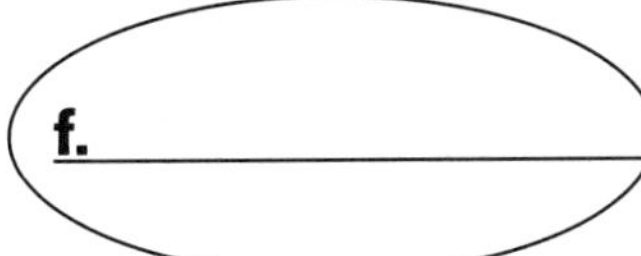

g. _______________   **h.** _______________

Chapter Test C

Formation of the Solar System
MULTIPLE CHOICE
Circle the letter of the best answer for each question.

1. What might sunspots affect on Earth?
   - **a.** electric fields
   - **b.** magnetic fields
   - **c.** temperatures
   - **d.** plant growth

2. What did planetesimals do to form Earth?
   - **a.** collapsed inward
   - **b.** orbited the sun
   - **c.** left the solar system
   - **d.** crashed and combined

3. What caused oceans to form when Earth cooled?
   - **a.** snow
   - **b.** rain
   - **c.** steam
   - **d.** glaciers

4. What happens if objects have more mass and move closer together?
   - **a.** Pressure increases.
   - **b.** Pressure decreases.
   - **c.** Gravity between them increases.
   - **d.** Gravity between them decreases.

5. What made the solar system form?
   - **a.** Gravity decreased.
   - **b.** Pressure decreased.
   - **c.** The solar nebula collapsed.
   - **d.** The solar nebula pulled together.

Chapter Test C *continued*

MULTIPLE CHOICE
Circle the letter of the best answer for each question.

6. What happened as light rocks rose to Earth's surface?

   a. Mountains formed.

   b. The oceans got larger.

   c. The mantle got lighter.

   d. Early continents formed.

7. How do planets move if they are closer to the sun?

   a. smoother

   b. rougher

   c. slower

   d. faster

8. What is used to find a planet's distance from the sun?

   a. the planet's mass

   b. the planet's size

   c. the planet's period of revolution

   d. the planet's number of moons

9. What gas was added to the atmosphere change as life-forms carried out photosynthesis?

   a. hydrogen.

   b. oxygen.

   c. sulfur.

   d. argon.

10. What process gives the sun its energy?

   a. photosynthesis

   b. cellular regeneration

   c. cellular fission

   d. nuclear fusion

MATCHING

Read the description. Then, <u>draw a line</u> from the dot next to each description to the matching word.

11. Earth's central layer   ●

12. the outer layer of Earth   ●

13. the middle layer of Earth   ●

a. crust

b. mantle

c. core

---

14. the spin of a planet on its axis   ●

15. one complete trip around the sun   ●

16. the path a planet follows when it travels around the sun   ●

17. shape of the path a planet follows when it travels around the sun   ●

a. ellipse

b. orbit

c. rotation

d. revolution

| Chapter Test C *continued*

FILL-IN-THE-BLANK

Read the words in the box. Read the sentences. <u>Fill in each blank</u> with the word or phrase that best completes the sentence.

solar nebula	pressure
photosphere	convective zone

18. Gravity and ________________________ must balance each other to hold a nebula together.

19. The solar system was formed from a cloud called the

________________________.

20. Gases circulate and carry energy to the sun's surface from the

________________________.

21. Energy leaves the sun from the layer we see called the

________________________.

Assessment)

Performance-Based Assessment

OBJECTIVE

In this activity, you will use colored sand to model the composition of Earth's atmosphere during its development.

KNOW THE SCORE!

As you work through the activity, keep in mind that you will be earning a grade for the following:

- how well you work with the materials (20%)
- the quality and clarity of your measurements (30%)
- how well you explain your observations (50%)

MATERIALS AND EQUIPMENT

- atmospheric data chart
- 100 mL graduated cylinders (3)
- 200 mL beakers full of colored sand (5): 1 red, 1 blue, 1 yellow, 1 green, 1 white

COLOR CODE

- **blue:** H_2O
- **red:** CO_2
- **green:** N_2
- **white:** O_2
- **yellow:** Ar

SAFETY INFORMATION 

- Be sure to wear safety goggles as you do the activity.
- Be very careful when handling glass materials. Inform your teacher immediately of any broken glass.

PROCEDURE

1. Examine the data chart. It details Earth's atmosphere during the three stages described in the chapter. Do you think the composition of the atmosphere in each phase is known for certain? Explain your answer.

____

____

Performance-Based Assessment *continued*

2. To model Earth's atmosphere in phase I, fill a graduated cylinder with 50 mL of blue sand (for the 50 percent water vapor) and 50 mL of red sand (for the 50 percent carbon dioxide). Sprinkle in a little green, white, and yellow sand to represent the trace amounts of nitrogen, oxygen, and argon.

3. Fill the second graduated cylinder with the correct amounts of blue, red, and green sand to model Earth's atmosphere in phase II. Add sprinkles of the other colors to represent the trace elements. How much of each color of sand did you use?

____

____

4. Fill the third graduated cylinder with colored sand to represent the current atmosphere. How much of each color of sand did you use?

____

____

ANALYSIS

5. What major changes took place in the atmosphere between phases I and II?

____

6. What major changes took place between phases II and III?

____

____

____

7. What most likely caused the change in the amount of water vapor between phases II and III? (Hint: What is more likely to bring rain—hot weather or cool weather?)

____

____

____

____

Standardized Test Preparation

READING

Read each of the passages below. Then, answer the questions that follow each passage.

Passage 1 You know that you should not look at the sun, right? But how can we learn anything about the sun if we can't look at it? We can use a solar telescope! About 70 km southwest of Tucson, Arizona, is Kitt Peak National Observatory, where you will find three solar telescopes. In 1958, Kitt Peak was chosen from more than 150 mountain sites to be the site for a national observatory. Located in the Sonoran Desert, Kitt Peak is on land belonging to the Tohono O'odham Indian nation. On this site, the McMath-Pierce Facility houses the three largest solar telescopes in the world. Astronomers come from around the globe to use these telescopes. The largest of the three, the McMath-Pierce solar telescope, produces an image of the sun that is almost 1 m wide!

_______ **1.** Which of the following is the largest telescope in the world?
   A Kitt Peak
   B Tohono O'odham
   C McMath-Pierce
   D Tucson

_______ **2.** According to the passage, how can you learn about the sun?
   F You can look at it.
   G You can study it by using a solar telescope.
   H You can go to Kitt Peak National Observatory.
   I You can study to be an astronomer.

_______ **3.** Which of the following is a fact in the passage?
   A One hundred fifty mountain sites contain solar telescopes.
   B Kitt Peak is the location of the smallest solar telescope in the world.
   C In 1958, Tucson, Arizona, was chosen for a national observatory.
   D Kitt Peak is the location of the largest solar telescope in the world.

Standardized Test Preparation *continued*

Passage 2 Sunlight that has been focused can produce a great amount of thermal energy—enough to start a fire. Now, imagine focusing the sun's rays by using a magnifying glass that is 1.6 m in diameter. The resulting heat could melt metal. If a <u>conventional</u> telescope were pointed directly at the sun, it would melt. To avoid a meltdown, the McMath-Pierce solar telescope uses a mirror that produces a large image of the sun. This -mirror directs the sun's rays down a diagonal shaft to another mirror, which is 50 m underground. This mirror is adjustable to focus the sunlight. The sunlight is then directed to a third mirror, which directs the light to an observing room and instrument shaft.

_______ **1.** In this passage, what does the word *conventional* mean?
   A special
   B solar
   C unusual
   D ordinary

_______ **2.** What can you infer from reading the passage?
   F Focused sunlight can avoid a meltdown.
   G Unfocused sunlight produces little energy.
   H A magnifying glass can focus sunlight to produce a great amount of thermal energy.
   I Mirrors increase the intensity of sunlight.

_______ **3.** According to the passage, which of the following statements about solar telescopes is true?
   A Solar telescopes make it safe for scientists to observe the sun.
   B Solar telescopes don't need to use mirrors.
   C Solar telescopes are built 50 m underground.
   D Solar telescopes are 1.6 m in diameter.

Standardized Test Preparation *continued*

INTERPRETING GRAPHICS

The diagram below models the moon's orbit around the Earth. Use the diagram below to answer the questions that follow.

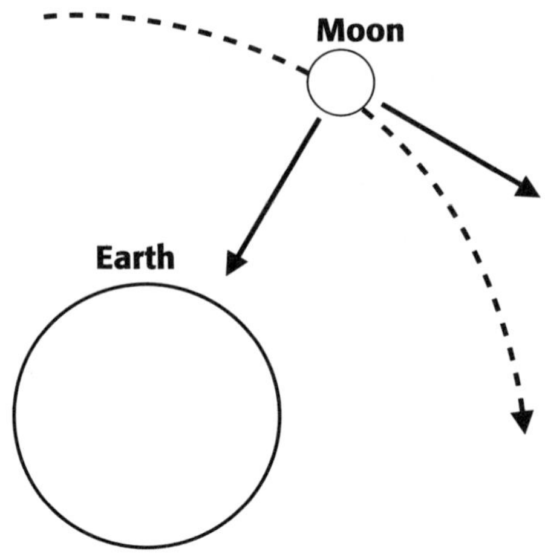

_______ **1.** Which statement best describes the diagram?
   A Orbits are straight lines.
   B The force of gravity does not affect orbits.
   C Orbits result from a combination of gravitational attraction and inertia.
   D The moon moves in three different directions depending on its speed.

_______ **2.** In which direction does gravity pull the moon?
   F toward the Earth
   G around the Earth
   H away from the Earth
   I toward and away from the Earth

_______ **3.** If the moon stopped moving, what would happen?
   A It would fly off into space.
   B It would continue to orbit the Earth.
   C It would stay where it is in space.
   D It would move toward the Earth.

| Standardized Test Preparation *continued*

MATH

Read each question below, and choose the best answer.

_______ **1.** An astronomer found 3 planetary systems in the nebula that she was studying. One system had 6 planets, another had 2 planets, and the third had 7 planets. What is the average number of planets in all 3 systems?
  A 3
  B 5
  C 8
  D 16

_______ **2.** A newly discovered planet has a period of rotation of 270 Earth years. How many Earth days are in 270 Earth years?
  F 3,240
  G 8,100
  H 9,855
  I 98,550

_______ **3.** A planet has seven rings. The first ring is 20,000 km from the center of the planet. Each ring is 50,000 km wide and 500 km apart. What is the total radius of the ring system from the planet's center?
  A 353,000 km
  B 373,000 km
  C 373,500 km
  D 370,000 km

_______ **4.** If you bought a telescope for $87.75 and received a $10 bill, two $1 bills, and a quarter as change, how much money did you give the clerk?
  F $100
  G $99
  H $98
  I $90

Skills Practice Lab

How Far Is the Sun?

It doesn't slice, it doesn't dice, but it can give you an idea of how big our universe is! You can build your very own solar-distance measuring device from household items. Amaze your friends by figuring out how many metersticks can be placed between the Earth and the sun.

OBJECTIVES

Create a solar-distance measuring device.

Calculate the Earth's distance from the sun.

MATERIALS

- aluminum foil, 5 cm × 5 cm
- card, index
- meterstick
- poster board

- ruler, metric
- scissors
- tape, masking
- thumbtack

SAFETY 

Using Scientific Methods

ASK A QUESTION

1. How many metersticks could I place between the Earth and the sun?

FORM A HYPOTHESIS

2. Write a hypothesis that answers the question above.

____

____

TEST THE HYPOTHESIS

3. Measure and cut a 4 cm × 4 cm square from the middle of the poster board. Tape the foil square over the hole in the center of the poster board.

4. Using a thumbtack, carefully prick the foil to form a tiny hole in the center. Congratulations! You have just constructed your very own solar-distance measuring device!

5. Tape the device to a window facing the sun so that sunlight shines directly through the pinhole. **Caution:** Do not look directly into the sun.

6. Place one end of the meterstick against the window and beneath the foil square. Steady the meterstick with one hand.

How Far Is the Sun? *continued*

7. With the other hand, hold the index card close to the pinhole. You should be able to see a circular image on the card. This image is an image of the sun.

8. Move the card back until the image is large enough to measure. Be sure to keep the image on the card sharply focused. Reposition the meterstick so that it touches the bottom of the card.

9. Ask your partner to measure the diameter of the image on the card by using the metric ruler. Record the diameter of the image in millimeters.

10. Record the distance between the window and the index card by reading the point at which the card rests on the meterstick.

11. Calculate the distance between Earth and the sun by using the following formula:

$$\text{distance between the sun and Earth} = \text{sun's diameter} \times \frac{\text{distance to the image}}{\text{image's diameter}}$$

1 cm = 10 mm
1 m = 100 cm
1 km = 1,000 m

(Hint: The sun's diameter is 1,392,000,000 m.)

ANALYZE THE RESULTS

1. Analyzing Results According to your calculations, how far from the Earth is the sun? Don't forget to convert your measurements to meters.

____

____

DRAW CONCLUSIONS

2. Evaluating Data You could put 150 billion metersticks between the Earth and the sun. Compare this information with your result in step 11. Do you think that this activity was a good way to measure the Earth's distance from the sun? Support your answer.

____

____

____

____

Quick Lab

Staying in Focus

MATERIALS

- string, about 12 cm long
- unlined paper
- 2 thumbtacks
- pencil

PROCEDURE:

1. Take a **short piece of string**, and pin both ends to a **piece of paper** with **two thumbtacks.**

2. Keep the string stretched tight at all times, use a **pencil** to trace out the path of the ellipse.

3. Change the Distance between the thumbtacks to change the shape of the ellipse.

4. How does the position of the thumbtacks (foci) affect the ellipse?

____

____

____

____

____

____

Activity

Vocabulary Activity

Formation of the Solar System

After you finish reading the chapter use the clues below to complete the crossword puzzle on the next page.

ACROSS

3. works with pressure to keep a nebula from collapsing

4. the layer of Earth that extends to its center

5. Kepler's three laws are about this.

8. The dense layer of the sun that blocks energy and light is the _____ zone.

9. the layer of the sun we see

11. came up with the formula $E = mc^2$

13. collided to form planets

16. one of the giant gas planets

17. the outermost layer of Earth

19. the shape of Earth's path around the sun

20. the path traveled by a planet around the sun

21. the outermost layer of the sun

23. Gravity depends on mass and the _____ between objects.

24. a cooler area on the sun's surface

DOWN

1. An eruption on the sun's surface is a solar _____.

2. the layer of the sun between the corona and the photosphere

4. Gases circulate in the _____ zone of the sun.

6. the process of absorbing energy from the sun and carbon dioxide from the atmosphere to make food

7. the middle layer of Earth

10. the movement of a planet around the sun

12. a huge, interstellar cloud of gas and dust

13. The time a planet takes to make a single trip around the sun is its _____ of revolution.

14. The cloud of gas and dust that formed our solar system is the _____ nebula.

15. The source of the sun's energy is nuclear _____.

18. the spinning of a planet on its axis

22. material that melted to form the early continents

▌Vocabulary Activity *continued*

SciLinks Activity

THE SUN

Go to www.scilinks.org. To find links related to the sun, type in the keyword HSM1477. Then, use the links to complete the following activity about the sun.

Imagine that you are a science journalist. Complete the article below about the sun. Add a title in the top box. Write information to go with each headline in the other boxes. Then, draw a picture in the bottom right box. Write a caption below the picture.

Introducing...the Sun!

Special Facts About the Sun

How the Sun Helps Us

Performance-Based Assessment

Teacher Notes and Answer Key

Paul Boyle
Perry Heights Middle School
Evansville, Indiana

PURPOSE
Students pour colored sand into graduated cylinders in order to visualize the composition of the Earth's atmosphere during different stages of its development.

TIME REQUIRED
One 45-minute class period.

RATINGS

Easy ← 1   2   3   4 → Hard

Teacher Prep–3
Student Set-Up–1
Concept Level–1
Clean Up–2

ADVANCE PREPARATION
Equip each activity station with the necessary materials, including a copy of the data chart below. Plain sand can be colored by adding food coloring to water, mixing the colored water into the sand, and then drying the sand in a shallow pan in an oven.

SAFETY INFORMATION 
Students should wear safety goggles. Have a sharps container available in case of glass breakage.

TEACHING STRATEGIES
This activity works best in groups of 2–3 students.

Historical Atmospheric Data

Gas	Percentage of Earth's Atmosphere		
	Phase I (4 billion years ago)	**Phase II** (2.5 billion years ago)	**Phase III** (present)
Water vapor (H_2O)	50%	50%	traces
Carbon dioxide (CO_2)	50%	30%	traces
Nitrogen (N_2)	traces	20%	78%
Oxygen (O_2)	traces	traces	21%
Argon (Ar)	traces	traces	1%

Performance-Based Assessment *continued*

Evaluation strategies

Use the following rubric to help evaluate student performance.

Rubric for Assessment

Possible points	Appropriate use of materials and equipment (20 points possible)
20–10	Correct use of measuring equipment; safe lab technique
9–1	Incorrect use of measuring equipment
	Quality and clarity of measurements (30 points possible)
30–20	Accurate sand measurements; correct gas-color correspondence
19–10	Basically accurate sand measurements; essentially correct gas-color correspondence, with minor mistakes
9–1	Inaccurate sand measurements; incorrect gas-color correspondence
	Interpretation of observations (50 points possible)
50–40	Clear, detailed answers showing superior grasp of chapter material relating to Earth's atmosphere; few or no mistakes
39–30	Complete answers showing solid grasp of main ideas; some minor mistakes in explanations
29–20	Complete answers showing elementary grasp of main ideas; some mistakes in details
19–10	Incomplete and/or wrong answers showing poor grasp of main ideas; many mistakes takes in details
9–1	Incomplete answers showing little or no knowledge of chapter concepts, or efforts to use them. many mistakes takes in details

Name _______________________________ Class _______________ Date ____________

 MODEL-MAKING

Performance-Based Assessment

OBJECTIVE

In this activity, you will use colored sand to model the composition of Earth's atmosphere during its development.

KNOW THE SCORE!

As you work through the activity, keep in mind that you will be earning a grade for the following:

- how well you work with the materials (20%)
- the quality and clarity of your measurements (30%)
- how well you explain your observations (50%)

MATERIALS AND EQUIPMENT

- atmospheric data chart
- 100 mL graduated cylinders (3)
- 200 mL beakers full of colored sand (5): 1 red, 1 blue, 1 yellow, 1 green, 1 white

COLOR CODE

- **blue:** H_2O
- **red:** CO_2
- **green:** N_2
- **white:** O_2
- **yellow:** Ar

SAFETY INFORMATION

- Be sure to wear safety goggles as you do the activity.
- Be very careful when handling glass materials. Inform your teacher immediately of any broken glass.

PROCEDURE

1. Examine the data chart. It details Earth's atmosphere during the three stages described in the chapter. Do you think the composition of the atmosphere in each phase is known for certain? Explain your answer.

   Answers may vary. Sample answer: No; the compositions for phases I and II

   must be guesses because it's not possible to obtain direct measurements.

Name _______________________________ Class _______________ Date _______________

Performance-Based Assessment *continued*

2. To model Earth's atmosphere in phase I, fill a graduated cylinder with 50 mL of blue sand (for the 50 percent water vapor) and 50 mL of red sand (for the 50 percent carbon dioxide). Sprinkle in a little green, white, and yellow sand to represent the trace amounts of nitrogen, oxygen, and argon.

3. Fill the second graduated cylinder with the correct amounts of blue, red, and green sand to model Earth's atmosphere in phase II. Add sprinkles of the other colors to represent the trace elements. How much of each color of sand did you use?

I used 50 mL of blue sand, 30 mL of red sand, 20 mL of green sand, and

sprinkles of white and yellow.

4. Fill the third graduated cylinder with colored sand to represent the current atmosphere. How much of each color of sand did you use?

I used 78 mL of green sand, 21 mL of white sand, 1 mL of yellow sand, and

sprinkles of blue and red.

ANALYSIS

5. What major changes took place in the atmosphere between phases I and II?

Some of the carbon dioxide had been replaced by nitrogen in phase II.

6. What major changes took place between phases II and III?

The water vapor and carbon dioxide almost disappeared, the nitrogen greatly

increased, and a lot of oxygen appeared, along with a little argon.

7. What most likely caused the change in the amount of water vapor between phases II and III? (Hint: What is more likely to bring rain—hot weather or cool weather?)

Answers may vary. Sample answer: Earth probably cooled, which caused the

water in the atmosphere to condense into liquid. This liquid became part of

Earth's oceans and lakes.

Skills Practice Lab)

DATASHEET FOR CHAPTER LAB

How Far Is the Sun?

Teacher Notes and Answer Key

Daniel Bugenhagen
Yutan Jr.–Sr. High
Yutan, Nebraska

TIME REQUIRED
One 45-minute class period

RATING

Easy ◄ 1   2   3   4 ► Hard

Teacher Prep–2
Student Set-Up–1
Concept Level–4
Clean Up–1

MATERIALS
The materials listed on the student page are enough for a group of 2 or 3 students.

SAFETY INFORMATION

- Remind students to review all safety cautions and icons before beginning this lab activity.

- Also caution students never to look directly at the sun.

PREPARATION NOTES
Conduct this activity on a sunny day. This lab works best in the late afternoon because the sun is lower in the sky. The sunlight should come through the window at an angle as close to perpendicular as possible. It may help to lower the blinds so that the sunlight will pass through a narrow opening. Some sample data are provided in the table on the bottom of the next page.

Name _________________________________ Class _______________ Date ____________

DATASHEET FOR CHAPTER LAB

How Far Is the Sun?

It doesn't slice, it doesn't dice, but it can give you an idea of how big our universe is! You can build your very own solar-distance measuring device from household items. Amaze your friends by figuring out how many metersticks can be placed between the Earth and the sun.

OBJECTIVES

Create a solar-distance measuring device.

Calculate the Earth's distance from the sun.

MATERIALS

- aluminum foil, 5 cm × 5 cm
- card, index
- meterstick
- poster board
- ruler, metric
- scissors
- tape, masking
- thumbtack

SAFETY 

Using Scientific Methods

ASK A QUESTION

1. How many metersticks could I place between the Earth and the sun?

FORM A HYPOTHESIS

2. Write a hypothesis that answers the question above.

____

____

TEST THE HYPOTHESIS

3. Measure and cut a 4 cm × 4 cm square from the middle of the poster board. Tape the foil square over the hole in the center of the poster board.

4. Using a thumbtack, carefully prick the foil to form a tiny hole in the center. Congratulations! You have just constructed your very own solar-distance measuring device!

5. Tape the device to a window facing the sun so that sunlight shines directly through the pinhole. **Caution:** Do not look directly into the sun.

6. Place one end of the meterstick against the window and beneath the foil square. Steady the meterstick with one hand.

Name _________________________ Class ______________ Date __________

How Far Is the Sun? *continued*

7. With the other hand, hold the index card close to the pinhole. You should be able to see a circular image on the card. This image is an image of the sun.

8. Move the card back until the image is large enough to measure. Be sure to keep the image on the card sharply focused. Reposition the meterstick so that it touches the bottom of the card.

9. Ask your partner to measure the diameter of the image on the card by using the metric ruler. Record the diameter of the image in millimeters.

10. Record the distance between the window and the index card by reading the point at which the card rests on the meterstick.

11. Calculate the distance between Earth and the sun by using the following formula:

$$\text{distance between the sun and Earth} = \text{sun's diameter} \times \frac{\text{distance to the image}}{\text{image's diameter}}$$

1 cm = 10 mm
1 m = 100 cm
1 km = 1,000 m

(Hint: The sun's diameter is 1,392,000,000 m.)

ANALYZE THE RESULTS

1. Analyzing Results According to your calculations, how far from the Earth is the sun? Don't forget to convert your measurements to meters.

Answers may vary. Based on the sample data, the sun is 148,944,000,000 m from the Earth. The sun is actually 149,600,000,000 m away.

DRAW CONCLUSIONS

2. Evaluating Data You could put 150 billion metersticks between the Earth and the sun. Compare this information with your result in step 11. Do you think that this activity was a good way to measure the Earth's distance from the sun? Support your answer.

Answers may vary. Accept all well-supported answers. According to the

sample data, the calculated value was within 0.5 percent of the actual value.

So this activity is generally a good way to measure the distance from the

Earth to the sun.

Name ________________________________   Class _______________   Date ___________

<table><tr><td>Quick Lab</td><td>DATASHEET FOR QUICK LAB</td></tr></table>

Staying in Focus

MATERIALS

- string, about 12 cm long
- unlined paper
- 2 thumbtacks
- pencil

PROCEDURE:

1. Take a **short piece of string**, and pin both ends to a **piece of paper** with **two thumbtacks.**

2. Keep the string stretched tight at all times, use a **pencil** to trace out the path of the ellipse.

3. Change the Distance between the thumbtacks to change the shape of the ellipse.

4. How does the position of the thumbtacks (foci) affect the ellipse?

   The closer together the foci are, the more circular the ellipse.

   ____

   ____

   ____

   ____

   ____

SAFETY CAUTION:

Students should use care with thumb-tacks to avoid injuring themselves or damaging the surface on which they work. Have them put a piece of cardboard under their sheet of paper.

Answer Key

Directed Reading A

SECTION: A SOLAR SYSTEM IS BORN

1. solar system
2. D
3. C
4. A
5. gravity
6. temperature
7. Outward pressure balances the inward gravitational pull and keeps the cloud from collapsing.
8. The balance between gravity and pressure in a nebula can be upset if two nebulas collide or if a star explodes.
9. globules
10. solar nebula
11. B
12. D
13. C
14. dust
15. planetesimals
16. nebula gases
17. Jupiter, Saturn, Uranus, Neptune
18. rocky
19. Mercury, Venus, Earth, Mars
20. helium
21. Our sun was born.
22. 4
23. 1
24. 6
25. 2
26. 5
27. 3

SECTION: THE SUN: OUR VERY OWN STAR

1. B
2. E
3. A
4. F
5. D
6. B
7. C
8. D
9. A
10. D
11. B
12. B
13. nuclear fusion
14. A helium nucleus and energy are produced.
15. core
16. radiative zone
17. convective zone
18. photosphere
19. D
20. Answers will vary. Sample answer: The sun's magnetic fields tend to slow down activity in the convective zone. When this activity slows down, areas of the photosphere become cooler than surrounding areas.
21. sunspots
22. 11
23. Answers will vary. Sample answer: Sunspots may affect climate. For example, scientists have linked very low sunspot activity with low temperatures.
24. solar flares
25. Solar flares can interrupt radio communications on Earth.

SECTION: THE EARTH TAKES SHAPE

1. C
2. A
3. C
4. D
5. B
6. Planetesimals that collided with one another and radioactive material.
7. Answers will vary. Sample answer: After Earth reached a certain size, the temperature rose faster than the interior could cool, and the rocky material inside began to melt.
8. core
9. crust
10. mantle
11. B
12. A
13. C
14. D
15. A
16. D
17. B
18. Water vapor from volcanic gases may have condensed to form the first oceans. The ice from comets may have also brought some of the water in the oceans.
19. ozone layer
20. molecules
21. life-forms
22. photosynthesis
23. oxygen

24. carbon dioxide
25. 2.2 billion years ago
26. D   **29.** 4
27. A   **30.** 3
28. 1   **31.** 2

SECTION: PLANETARY MOTION

1. As Earth rotates, one-half of Earth faces the sun. The half that faces the sun is day. The half that is away from the sun is night.
2. B
3. D
4. A
5. C
6. ellipse
7. major axis
8. semimajor axis
9. The closer a planet is to the sun, the faster it moves around the sun.
10. The planet's period of revolution.
11. A
12. D
13. D
14. C
15. C

Directed Reading B

SECTION: A SOLAR SYSTEM IS BORN

1. D   **10.** solar nebula
2. D   **11.** C
3. C   **12.** D
4. A   **13.** A
5. C   **14.** B
6. A   **15.** C
7. temperature **16.** A
8. pressure   **17.** D
9. globules   **18.** C

SECTION: THE SUN: OUR VERY OWN STAR

1. C   **12.** D
2. B   **13.** core
3. C   **14.** radiative zone
4. A   **15.** convective zone
5. A   **16.** photosphere
6. C   **17.** D
7. B   **18.** B
8. D   **19.** A
9. C   **20.** C
10. B   **21.** B
11. A   **22.** C

SECTION: THE EARTH TAKES SHAPE

1. A   **14.** C
2. A   **15.** C
3. D   **16.** C
4. B   **17.** A
5. B   **18.** B
6. C   **19.** B
7. A   **20.** A
8. C   **21.** C
9. B   **22.** B
10. A   **23.** A
11. D   **24.** D
12. D   **25.** A
13. B

SECTION: PLANETARY MOTION

1. C   **7.** C
2. B   **8.** D
3. D   **9.** A
4. A   **10.** B
5. B   **11.** A
6. D

Vocabulary and Section Summary

SECTION: A SOLAR SYSTEM IS BORN

1. nebula: a large cloud of gas and dust in interstellar space; a region in space where stars are born or where stars explode at the end of their lives
2. solar nebula: the cloud of gas and dust that formed our solar system

SECTION: THE SUN: OUR VERY OWN STAR

1. nuclear fusion: the combination of the nuclei of small atoms to form a larger nucleus; releases energy
2. sunspot: a dark area of the photosphere of the sun that is cooler than the surrounding areas and that has a strong magnetic field

SECTION: THE EARTH TAKES SHAPE

1. crust: the thin and solid outermost layer of the Earth above the mantle
2. mantle: the layer of rock between the Earth's crust and core
3. core: the central part of the Earth below the mantle

SECTION: PLANETARY MOTION

1. rotation: the spin of a body on its axis
2. orbit: the path that a body follows as it travels around another body in space
3. revolution: the motion of a body that travels around another body in space; one complete trip along an orbit

Section Review

SECTION: A SOLAR SYSTEM IS BORN

1. Sample answer: A nebula is a large cloud of gas and dust in interstellar space. The solar nebula is the cloud of gas and dust that formed our solar system.
2. B
3. Sample answer: After the balance between gravity and pressure became unbalanced in the solar nebula, the solar nebula began to collapse. The solar nebula became denser and the attraction between the gas and dust particles increased. This caused the center of the nebula to become dense and hot. Therefore, as bits of dust circled the center, some collided to form planetesimals. The central mass of the nebula became the sun, and the planetesimals that continued to circle the sun eventually combined to form the planets.
4. The inner planets, Mercury, Venus, Earth, and Mars, formed closer to the sun where temperatures were too hot for gases to remain and therefore are made up of mostly rocky material. The outer planets, Jupiter, Saturn, Uranus, and Neptune, formed farther from the sun and are partially made up of gases.
5. 99.85%
6. Answers will vary.
7. Answers will vary. Sample answer: The planets formed from the flattened disk of the nebula, which rotated in one direction. The dust and gas that formed the planets moved in the same direction that the nebula was spinning.

SECTION: THE SUN: OUR VERY OWN STAR

1. Sample answer: A sunspot is a dark area of the photosphere of the sun that is cooler than the surrounding areas. Nuclear fusion is the combination of the nuclei of small atoms to form a larger nucleus.
2. B
3. The sun is a large ball of gas made up of mostly hydrogen and helium held together by gravity.
4. The corona forms the sun's outer atmosphere. The chromosphere is a thin region below the corona, only 30,000 km thick. The photosphere is the visible part of the sun that we can see from Earth. The convective zone is a region about 200,000 km thick where gases circulate. The radiative zone is a very dense region about 300,000 km thick. The core is at the center of the sun, where the sun's energy is produced.
5. Sunspots appear as cooler, dark spots of the photosphere of the sun.
6. The sun's magnetic fields slow down the activity in the convective zone, which causes areas of the photosphere to become cooler. Sunspots are the dark, cool spots on the sun.
7. Sample answer: Scientists think that a period of low sunspot activity may cause lower temperatures on Earth.
8. Solar flares are regions of extremely high temperature and brightness that develop on the sun's surface. Solar flares are caused by the sun's magnetic fields, which are caused by the movement of energy in the sun.
9. $1,390,000 \text{ km} \div 2 = 695,000 \text{ km}$
10. No, it would take millions of years for the last energy made in the core to reach the surface of the sun.

11. In the 19th century, some scientists thought that the sun burned fuel to generate its energy. Other scientists thought that gravity was causing the sun to slowly shrink and release energy. Finally, with the help of Albert Einstein's equation, $E = mc^2$, the process of nuclear fusion was defined. Nuclear fusion is the combination of the nuclei of small atoms to form a large nucleus. The result of nuclear fusion is the release of a large amount of energy. The fusion of hydrogen into helium in the sun generates a large amount of energy and therefore is the source of the sun's energy.

SECTION: THE EARTH TAKES SHAPE

1. Sample answer: The crust is the thin and solid outermost layer of Earth above the mantle. The mantle is the layer of rock between Earth's crust and core. The core is below the mantle and is the central part of Earth.
2. C
3. Earth is divided into three layers: the crust, the mantle, and the core. The crust is the thin, outermost layer, the mantle is the layer of Earth beneath the crust; and the core is the central and densest part of Earth.
4. As rocks melted inside Earth, denser materials sank to the center of Earth, and less dense materials floated to the surface.
5. Sample answer: Scientists think that Earth's first atmosphere contained carbon dioxide and water vapor. Later, volcanoes added carbon dioxide, water vapor, chlorine, nitrogen, and sulfur. Comets brought water, carbon, hydrogen, nitrogen, and oxygen. Solar energy created new chemicals that led to the formation of living organisms. These organisms greatly changed the composition of the atmosphere by adding oxygen.

6. Scientists think that the oceans formed when Earth was cool enough for rain to fall and remain on the surface. After millions of years of rainfall, water began to cover Earth and eventually formed the global ocean. Earth's continents formed as heavy elements sank close to the core of Earth and light elements rose to Earth's surface. The light elements were light enough to pile up on the surface and began to form the earliest continents. The continents gradually thickened and slowly rose above the surface of the ocean.
7. When Earth was still a young planet, it had an irregular shape. But as Earth gained more matter, gravity became greater than the strength of the rock. Therefore, the rock at the center of Earth was crushed by gravity and Earth started to become round.
8. Answers will vary. Deforestation on a large scale would allow more carbon dioxide to accumulate in the atmosphere. As carbon dioxide increased, oxygen levels would likely decrease.
9. B
10. C

SECTION: PLANETARY MOTION

1. Sample answer: Revolution is the motion of a body that travels around another body in space. Rotation is the spin of a body on its own axis.
2. B
3. mass and distance
4. The motion of a planet is balanced between falling toward the sun and moving in a straight line past the sun. The resultant path is a curved orbit around the sun.
5. 365.25 days $\times$ 24 h = 8,766 h
6. The closer moon would finish first. Kepler's third law states that period of revolution is related to the distance of an orbiting body from the object it orbits (its semimajor axis). A closer object has a shorter period of revolution.

7. Kepler's first law of motion states that orbits are elliptical. Kepler's second law of motion states that planets move faster when they are closer to the sun and slower when they are farther from the sun. Kepler's third law explains the relationship between the period of a planet's revolution and its semimajor axis. Kepler's three laws allowed him to understand how a planet orbits the sun and how to calculate its distance from the sun.

Chapter Review

1. nebula

2. mantle

3. Answers will vary. Sample answer: A nebula is a large cloud of gas and dust in interstellar space. The solar nebula is the cloud of gas and dust that formed our solar system.

4. Answers will vary. Sample answer: The crust is the thin and solid outermost layer of Earth above the mantle. The mantle is the layer of rock between Earth's crust and core.

5. Answers will vary. Sample answer: Rotation is the spin of a body on its axis. Revolution is the motion of a body that travels around another body in space.

6. Answers will vary. Sample answer: Nuclear fusion is the combination of the nuclei of small atoms to form a larger nucleus. A sunspot is a dark area of the photosphere of the sun that is cooler than the surrounding areas and that has a strong magnetic field.

7. C

8. B

9. C

10. D

11. C

12. C

13. B

14. B

15. A

16. Answers will vary. Sample answer: A sunspot is a dark area of the photosphere of the sun that is cooler than the surrounding areas and that has a strong magnetic field. A solar flare is a region of extremely high temperature and brightness that develops on the sun's surface.

17. Answers will vary. Sample answer: Scientists think that the oceans formed during Earth's second atmosphere, when the Earth was cool enough for rain to fall. After millions of years of rainfall, the water began to cover Earth, which eventually formed a global ocean. The continents formed after the first few hundred million years and are made up of rocks that have melted and cooled many times.

18. Answers will vary. Sample answer: Pressure and gravity may have become unbalanced in the solar nebula because of an external force from a collision with another nebula or from a nearby exploding star. This force was strong enough to overcome the pressure of the nebula and trigger its collapse.

19. Answers will vary. Sample answer: Nuclear fusion is the combination of the nuclei of small atoms to form a larger nucleus. In the core of the sun, the temperature and pressure are very high. Therefore, the hydrogen nuclei, which would normally repel each other, have enough energy to overcome the repulsive force to fuse into helium. This fusion releases a large amount of energy, which leaves the sun as light to eventually reach Earth.

20. An answer to this exercise can be found at the end of the book.

21. Answers will vary. Sample answer: Kepler could describe planetary orbits, but he could not explain why planets stay in their orbits. Newton's law of gravitation explained why the planets orbit the sun.

22. Answers will vary. Sample answer: Photosynthesizing organisms released oxygen into the atmosphere. Some of this oxygen formed the ozone layer. The ozone layer shielded Earth from most of the sun's harmful UV radiation and allowed more complex life-forms to develop. If the ozone layer is damaged, some types of organisms could be threatened.

23. Answers will vary. Sample answer: Kepler's first law of motion states that an ellipse is a closed curve in which the sum of the distances from the edge of the curve to two points inside the ellipse is always the same. Kepler's second law of motion states that planets move faster when they are closer to the sun and slower when they are farther from the sun. Kepler's third law explains the relationship between the period of a planet's revolution and its semimajor axis.

24. Kepler's first law of motion

25. Answers will vary. Sample answer: The equation supports the law because the law states that an ellipse is a closed curve in which the sum of the distances from the edge of the curve to two points inside the ellipse is always the same. Therefore, a + b = c + d.

26. major axis

Reinforcement

STAY ON THE SUNNY SIDE

Answers from innermost to outermost layer: core, radiative zone, convective zone, photosphere, chromosphere, corona.

1. photosphere
2. radiative zone
3. corona
4. chromosphere
5. core
6. convective zone

THIRD ROCK FROM THE SUN

1. 4.6 billion years ago: Earth forms.
4 billion years ago: A global ocean covers Earth.
3.4 billion years ago: Organisms carry out photosynthesis.
2.5 billion years ago: Continents start to grow.
2.2 billion years ago: Simple plants move onto land.
1.5 billion years ago: The upper mantle becomes heavier.

2. As organisms made food through photosynthesis, more oxygen was added to the atmosphere. At the same time, carbon dioxide was removed from the atmosphere.

Critical Thinking

1. Answers will vary. Sample answer: No, Walter P. Balooney's explanation is not logical. Even if our solar system is the only one in which life exists, that does not mean that it formed differently.

2. Answers will vary. Sample answer: Yes; his theory relies on the assumption that life cannot possibly exist in any solar system other than our own.

3. Answers will vary. Sample answer: Yes, his argument shows bias. He believes that too much tax money is spent on solar system research.

4. Answers will vary. Sample answer: He says that Mercury's orbit was the cause of gravity, but it really is an effect of gravity.

5. Answers will vary. Sample answer: Gravity affects all bodies in the universe. Therefore, the planets should have been attracted to the stars nearest to them, not to our sun.

6. Answers will vary. Sample answer: Mr. Balooney's theory does not explain how the planets or the sun were formed.

Section Quizzes

SECTION: A SOLAR SYSTEM IS BORN

1. E	**6.** C
2. D	**7.** B
3. F	**8.** C
4. B	**9.** A
5. A	**10.** C

SECTION: THE SUN: OUR VERY OWN STAR

1. C	**6.** I
2. J	**7.** B
3. H	**8.** G
4. F	**9.** E
5. A	**10.** D

SECTION: THE EARTH TAKES SHAPE

1. D	**6.** C
2. C	**7.** A
3. A	**8.** B
4. D	**9.** B
5. C	

SECTION: PLANETARY MOTION

1. C	**6.** B
2. B	**7.** C
3. D	**8.** D
4. A	**9.** A
5. B	**10.** D

Chapter Test A

1. I	**14.** C
2. B	**15.** C
3. G	**16.** B
4. H	**17.** A
5. C	**18.** C
6. E	**19.** D
7. J	**20.** C
8. A	**21.** A
9. D	**22.** D
10. F	**23.** D
11. B	**24.** C
12. D	**25.** A
13. A	

Chapter Test B

1. crust
2. nebula
3. fusion
4. sunspot
5. rotation
6. C
7. A
8. C
9. B
10. D
11. Answers will vary. Sample answer: Kepler's first law of motion states that all planets move around the sun in elliptical orbits. Kepler's second law states that planets move faster when they are closer to the sun. Kepler's third law states that if a planet's period of revolution is known, the planet's distance from the sun can be calculated.
12. Answers will vary. Sample answer: When the inside of early Earth had melted, gravity caused the heavier elements, like nickel and iron, to sink to the center. Lighter elements floated to the surface. Over time, this process cause Earth to separate into layers.
13. Answers will vary. Sample answer: As particles in a nebula collide and move away from each other, pressure is created. The outward pressure balances the inward gravitational pull, and the nebula becomes stable.
14. Answers will vary. Sample answer: Planets were affected by their distance to the sun as they formed. For example, planetesimals that formed near the outside of the solar nebula attracted nebula gases. As a result, they're abundant in hydrogen and helium. Planets that formed near the center of thc ncbula were too hot to attract gases, so they are mostly made of rock.
15. Answers will vary. Sample answer: Planets are shaped like spheres because gravity pulls all of their material toward the center with equal force. In a sphere, each point on the surface is the same distance from the center.
16. Answers will vary. Sample answer: If large areas of forest are lost, there might not be as much oxygen in the atmosphere. The amount of carbon dioxide in the atmosphere might also increase.
17. Answers will vary. Sample answer: The most sunspots were recorded around the year 1778, and the fewest were recorded in the year 1810. About 32 years passed between the years of highest and lowest sunspot activity.
18. **a.** solar system; **b.** nebula; **c.** gravity; **d.** solar nebula; **e.** planetesimals; **f.** planets; **g.** rock; **h.** gas

Chapter Test C

1. C	**10.** D
2. D	**11.** C
3. B	**12.** A
4. C	**13.** B
5. C	**14.** C
6. D	**15.** D
7. D	**16.** B
8. C	**17.** A
9. B	**18.** pressure

19. solar nebula
20. convection zone
21. photosphere

Standardized Test Preparation

READING

Passage 1
  1. C
  2. G
  3. D

Passage 2
  1. D
  2. H
  3. A

INTERPRETING GRAPHICS
  1. C
  2. F
  3. B

MATH
  1. B
  2. H
  3. B
  4. F

Vocabulary Activity

ACROSS
  3. gravity
  4. core
  5. motion
  8. radiative
  9. photosphere
 11. Einstein
 13. planetesimals
 16. Saturn
 17. crust
 19. ellipse
 20. orbit
 21. corona
 23. distance
 24. sunspot

DOWN
  1. flare
  2. chromosphere
  4. convective
  6. photosynthesis
  7. mantle
 10. revolution
 12. nebula

13. period
14. solar
15. fusion
18. rotation
22. rock

SciLinks Activity

Answers will vary. Information in each section of the article should support the main idea as suggested by the headings. Students' picture may reflect any piece of information included in the article. The caption should summarize the information featured in the picture.

Lesson Plan

Section: A Solar System Is Born

Pacing

Regular Schedule: **with lab(s):** N/A   **without lab(s):** 1 day

Block Schedule: **with lab(s):** N/A   **without lab(s):** 0.5 day

Objectives

1. Explain the relationship between gravity and pressure in a nebula.

2. Describe how the solar system formed.

National Science Education Standards Covered

UCP 1: Systems, order, and organization

UCP 2: Evidence, models, and explanation

UCP 4: Evolution and equilibrium

ST 2: Understandings about science and technology

HNS 2: Nature of science

HNS 3: History of science

SPSP 5: Science and technology in society

ES 3a: The Earth is the third planet from the sun in a system that includes the moon, the sun, eight other planets and their moons, and smaller objects, such as asteroids and comets. The sun, an average star, is the central and largest body in the solar system.

ES 3b: Most objects in the solar system are in regular and predictable motion. Those motions explain such phenomena as the day, the year, the phases of the moon, and eclipses.

ES 3c: Gravity is the force that keeps planets in orbit around the sun and governs the rest of the motion in the solar system. Gravity alone holds us to the Earth's surface and explains the phenomena of the tides.

KEY

SE = Student Edition   **TE** = Teacher's Edition

CRF = Chapter Resource File

Lesson Plan

FOCUS *(5 minutes)*

_ **Chapter Starter Transparency** Use this transparency to introduce the chapter.

_ **Bellringer, TE** Have students discuss whether astronauts can land on a star in the same way that they land on the moon.

_ **Bellringer Transparency** Use this transparency as students enter the classroom and find their seats.

MOTIVATE *(10 minutes)*

_ **Group Activity, The Solar System, TE** Have students brainstorm facts they know about the solar system and questions they want answered. **(GENERAL)**

TEACH *(20 minutes)*

_ **Reading Strategy, Reading Organizer, SE** Have students make a flowchart of the steps of the formation of the solar system.

_ **Discussion, Reaching Equilibrium, TE** Have volunteers describe examples where gravity and pressure balance each other. **(BASIC)**

_ **Connection to Physical Science, Gas Laws, TE** Have students discuss Boyle's and Charles's laws. **(GENERAL)**

_ **Using the Figure, Forces in a Nebula, TE** Students use Figure 2 to explain the forces a of gravity and pressure. **(BASIC)**

_ **Inclusion Strategies, TE** Students use Figure 2 to explain the forces a of gravity and pressure. **(BASIC)**

_ **Activity, Planetesimal Formation, TE** Students model what the very early solar system would have looked like as predicted by the accretion theory.

_ **Directed Reading A/B, CRF** These worksheets reinforce basic concepts and vocabulary presented in the lesson. **(BASIC/SPECIAL NEEDS)**

_ **Vocabulary and Section Summary, CRF** Students write definitions of key terms and read a summary of section content. **(GENERAL)**

_ **Critical Thinking, A Balooney Solar System, CRF** Ask students to fill out the worksheet about a different theory that explains the formation of the solar system. **(ADVANCED)**

CLOSE *(10 minutes)*

_ **Homework, Preparing a Presentation, TE** Have students find information about the asteroid belt, the Kuiper belt, the Oort cloud, and comets. **(ADVANCED)**

_ **Reteaching, Stages of Formation, TE** Have students help sketch stages of solar-system formation. **(BASIC)**

_ **Quiz, TE** Students answer 2 questions about the formation of the sun and planets. **(GENERAL)**

_ **Alternative Assessment, Explaining How the Solar System Formed, TE** Students write a story in their journal explaining how the sun and planets formed. **(GENERAL)**

_ **Section Review, CRF** Students answer end-of-section vocabulary, key ideas, math, and critical thinking questions. **(GENERAL)**

_ **Section Quiz, CRF** Students answer 10 objective questions about how the solar system formed. **(GENERAL)**

Lesson Plan

Section: The Sun: Our Very Own Star

Pacing

Regular Schedule:	**with lab(s):** 2 days	**without lab(s):** 1 day
Block Schedule:	**with lab(s):** 1 day	**without lab(s):** 0.5 day

Objectives

1. Describe the basic structure and composition of the sun.

2. Explain how the sun generates energy.

3. Describe the surface activity of the sun, and identify how this activity affects Earth.

National Science Education Standards Covered

ST 2: Understandings about science and technology

SPSP 5: Science and technology in society

HNS 1: Science as a human endeavor

HNS 2: Nature of science

HNS 3: History of science

ES 3a: The Earth is the third planet from the sun in a system that includes the moon, the sun, eight other planets and their moons, and smaller objects, such as asteroids and comets. The sun, an average star, is the central and largest body in the solar system.

KEY

SE = Student Edition   **TE** = Teacher's Edition
CRF = Chapter Resource File

FOCUS (*5 minutes*)

Bellringer, TE Have students write about a quotation that references the sun.

Bellringer Transparency Use this transparency as students enter the classroom and find their seats.

MOTIVATE (*10 minutes*)

Demonstration, Observing Sunspots, TE Have students identify sunspots and other features of the sun. (**GENERAL**)

TEACH *(65 minutes)*

_ **Reading Strategy, Reading Organizer, SE** Have students create an outline of the section as they read.

_ **Using the Figure, The Structure of the Sun, TE** Students find dictionary definitions used in Figure 1. (**GENERAL**)

_ **Connection Activity Math, Graphing, TE** Students create a line graph showing the temperature of the sun's layer. (**GENERAL**)

_ **Group Activity, Escape from the Sun, TE** Students form groups to create a board game about the sun. (**ADVANCED**)

_ **Connection to Physical Science, Star Stuff, TE** Discuss with students the elements found in stars. (**GENERAL**)

_ **Connection Activity, History, TE** Have students explore information about the discoveries of Gerard Peter Kuiper. (**GENERAL**)

_ **Connection Activity Math, Graphing Density, TE** Students create a graph that compares the densities of the planet. (**BASIC**)

_ **Directed Reading A/B, CRF** These worksheets reinforce basic concepts and vocabulary presented in the lesson. (**BASIC/SPECIAL NEEDS**)

_ **Vocabulary and Section Summary, CRF** Students write definitions of key terms and read a summary of section content. (**GENERAL**)

_ **Reinforcement, Stay on the Sunny Side, CRF** This worksheet reinforces key concepts in the chapter. (**GENERAL**)

_ **SciLinks Activity, The Sun, SciLinks code HSM1477, CRF** Students research Internet resources related to the sun. (**GENERAL**)

_ **Chapter Lab, How Far Is the Sun?, SE** Students use a diagram to measure the distance from Earth to the sun. (**GENERAL**)

_ **Datasheet for Chapter Lab, How Far Is the Sun?, CRF** Students use the datasheet to complete the Chapter Lab. (**GENERAL**)

_ **Teaching Transparency, The Structure and Atmosphere of the Sun:** Use this graphic to review the composition of the sun.

_ **Teaching Transparency, Fusion of Hydrogen in the Sun** Use this graphic to review how the sun makes energy.

_ **Teaching Transparency, The Periodic Table of the Elements: Link to Physical Science** Use this graphic to discuss the types of elements that exist in the solar system.

CLOSE *(10 minutes)*

_ **Reteaching, The Layers of the Sun's Atmosphere, TE** Have students create a mnemonic device that helps them remember the sun's layers. **(BASIC)**

_ **Quiz, TE** Students answer 2 questions about the sun's energy. **(GENERAL)**

_ **Alternative Assessment, Energy Transfer, TE** Students explain how energy produced by nuclear fusion eventually reaches Earth. **(ADVANCED)**

_ **Section Review, CRF** Students answer end-of-section vocabulary, key ideas, math, and critical thinking questions. **(GENERAL)**

_ **Section Quiz, CRF** Students answer 10 objective questions about the sun. **(GENERAL)**

Lesson Plan

Section: The Earth Takes Shape

Pacing

Regular Schedule: **with lab(s):** N/A **without lab(s):** 1 day

Block Schedule: **with lab(s):** N/A **without lab(s):** 0.5 day

Objectives

1. Describe the formation of the solid Earth.

2. Describe the structure of the Earth.

3. Explain the development of Earth's atmosphere and the influence of early life on the atmosphere.

4. Describe how the Earth's oceans and continents formed.

National Science Education Standards Covered

UCP 2: Evidence, models, and explanation

UCP 4: Evolution and equilibrium

SAI 1: Abilities necessary to do scientific inquiry

ES 2b: Fossils provide important evidence of how life and environmental conditions have changed.

KEY

SE = Student Edition **TE** = Teacher's Edition

CRF = Chapter Resource File

FOCUS *(5 minutes)*

_ **Bellringer Transparency** Use this transparency as students enter the classroom and find their seats.

MOTIVATE *(10 minutes)*

_ **Discussion, Earth's Atmosphere, TE** Students speculate why there is very little hydrogen or helium in our atmosphere. **(GENERAL)**

Lesson Plan

TEACH *(20 minutes)*

_ **Reading Strategy, Discussion, SE** Ask students to write down questions they formed as they read the section.

_ **Connection Activity, Geology TE** Have students compare the densities of Mars and Earth. (**ADVANCED**)

_ **Reading Strategy, Earth's Atmosphere, TE** Have students speculate why there is very little hydrogen or helium in the atmosphere. (**GENERAL**)

_ **Inclusion Strategies, TE** Have students model the early interior of the Earth. (**GENERAL**)

_ **Connection to Life Science, The Presence of Oxygen, TE** Discuss with students oxygen's role in the atmosphere. (**GENERAL**)

_ **Internet Activity, Researching New Planets, TE** Have students research a planet orbiting outside of our solar system on the Internet. (**ADVANCED**)

_ **Debate, Life on Earth: Could It Happen Again?, TE** Ask students to debate whether life could evolve again with our current atmosphere. (**GENERAL**)

_ **Directed Reading A/B, CRF** These worksheets reinforce basic concepts and vocabulary presented in the lesson. (**BASIC/SPECIAL NEEDS**)

_ **Vocabulary and Section Summary, CRF** Students write definitions of key terms and read a summary of section content. (**GENERAL**)

_ **Reinforcement, Third Rock from the Sun, CRF** This worksheet reinforces key concepts in the chapter. (**GENERAL**)

_ **Teaching Transparency, Formation of Earth's Layers** Use this graphic to help students review how Earth's layers formed.

CLOSE *(10 minutes)*

_ **Homework, Poster Project, TE** Have students keep a record of the phases of the moon. (**GENERAL**)

_ **Section Review, CRF** Students answer end-of-section vocabulary, key ideas, critical thinking and interpreting graphics questions. (**GENERAL**)

_ **Section Quiz, CRF** Students answer 9 objective questions about the development of the Earth. (**GENERAL**)

_ **Reteaching, Changing Earth's Composition, TE** Have students discuss Earth's atmosphere. (**BASIC**)

_ **Quiz, TE** Students answer 3 questions about the formation of stars and Earth's atmosphere.

_ **Alternative Assessment, Earth Quiz Game, TE** Have students write a story that explains how the sun and the planets formed. (**GENERAL**)

Lesson Plan

Section: Planetary Motion

Pacing

Regular Schedule: **with lab(s):** N/A   **without lab(s):** 1 day

Block Schedule: **with lab(s):** N/A   **without lab(s):** 0.5 day

Objectives

1. Explain the difference between rotation and revolution.

2. Describe three laws of planetary motion.

3. Describe how distance and mass affect gravitational attraction.

National Science Education Standards Covered

UCP 1: Systems, order, and organization

UCP 2: Evidence, models, and explanation

UCP 3: Change, constancy, and measurement

SAI 1: Abilities necessary to do scientific inquiry

SAI 2: Understandings about scientific inquiry

ST 2: Understandings about science and technology

SPSP 5: Science and technology in society

HNS 1: Science as a human endeavor

HNS 2: Nature of science

HNS 3: History of science

ES 3b: Most objects in the solar system are in regular and predictable motion. Those motions explain such phenomena as the day, the year, the phases of the moon, and eclipses.

KEY

SE = Student Edition   **TE** = Teacher's Edition

CRF = Chapter Resource File

FOCUS *(5 minutes)*

_ **Bellringer Transparency**   Use this transparency as students enter the classroom and find their seats.

Lesson Plan

MOTIVATE *(5 minutes)*

_ **Activity, Measuring Ellipses, TE** Have students measure the segments of an ellipse to test Kepler's first law of motion. **(GENERAL)**

TEACH *(20 minutes)*

_ **Reading Strategy, Paired Summarizing, SE** Have students work with partners to summarize material in the section.

_ **Connection to Astronomy, The Moon's Orbit, TE** Discuss with students the condition of free fall on the moon. **(GENERAL)**

_ **Connection Activity, Language Arts, TE** Have students compose a letter to Johannes Kepler explaining planetary orbits. **(GENERAL)**

_ **Directed Reading A/B, CRF** These worksheets reinforce basic concepts and vocabulary presented in the lesson. **(BASIC/SPECIAL NEEDS)**

_ **Vocabulary and Section Summary, CRF** Students write definitions of key terms and read a summary of section content. **(GENERAL)**

_ **Quick Lab, Staying in Focus, SE** Students use string to trace out the path of an ellipse. **(GENERAL)**

_ **Datasheet for Quick Lab, Staying in Focus, CRF** This datasheet guides students through the Quick Lab. **(GENERAL)**

_ **Teaching Transparency, Earth's Rotation and Revolution** Use this graphic to help students learn about Earth's rotation and revolution.

_ **Teaching Transparency, Ellipse** Use this graphic to help students understand ellipses.

_ **Teaching Transparency, Gravity and Motion of the Moon** Use this graphic to discuss the relationship between gravity and the moon.

CLOSE *(10 minutes)*

_ **Reteaching, Comparing Kepler and Newton, TE** Have students compare the work of Kepler and Newton.

_ **Quiz, TE** Students answer 2 questions relating to Kepler's laws of planetary motion.

_ **Alternative Assessment, The Laws of Motion and Gravity, TE** Have students reproduce Figures 2, 3, 4, and 5 in their science journals.

_ **Section Review, CRF** Students answer end-of-section vocabulary, key ideas, math, and critical thinking questions. **(GENERAL)**

_ **Section Quiz, CRF** Students answer 10 objective questions about planetary motion. **(GENERAL)**

Lesson Plan

End of Chapter Review and Assessment

Pacing

Regular Schedule: **with lab(s):** N/A **without lab(s):** 2 days

Block Schedule: **with lab(s):** N/A **without lab(s):** 1 day

---

KEY

SE = Student Edition **TE** = Teacher's Edition
CRF = Chapter Resource File

_ **Chapter Review, CRF** Students answer end-of-chapter vocabulary, key ideas, critical thinking, and graphics questions. (**GENERAL**)

_ **Vocabulary Activity, CRF** Students review chapter vocabulary terms by working through a crossword puzzle. (**GENERAL**)

_ **Concept Mapping Transparency, TE** Use this graphic to help students review key concepts.

_ **Chapter Test A/B/C, CRF** Assign questions from the appropriate test for chapter assessment. (**GENERAL/ADVANCED/SPECIAL NEEDS**)

_ **Performance-Based Assessment, CRF** Assign this activity for general level assessment for the chapter. (**GENERAL**)

_ **Standardized Test Preparation, CRF** Students answer reading comprehension, math, and interpreting graphics questions in the format of a standardized test. (**GENERAL**)

_ **Test Generator, One-Stop Planner** Create a customized homework assignment, quiz, or test using the HRW Test Generator program. (**GENERAL**)

Formation of the Solar System

MULTIPLE CHOICE

1. A nebula is held together by the balance of
   a. the outward force of gravity and inward pressure.
   b. the inward force of gravity and outward pressure.
   c. high and low kinetic energies.
   d. high and low temperatures.
   Answer: B   Difficulty: 1   Section: 1   Objective: 1

2. After the solar nebula collapsed, its center became very hot and
   a. more nebulas formed.
   b. it formed into a sphere.
   c. planetesimals formed.
   d. it exploded.
   Answer: C   Difficulty: 1   Section: 1   Objective: 2

3. Planets began to form as
   a. planetesimals collided and combined.
   b. planetesimals flattened into rotating disks.
   c. temperatures in the solar nebula fell.
   d. gravity held together the solar nebula.
   Answer: A   Difficulty: 1   Section: 1   Objective: 2

4. The extra matter at the center of the solar nebula became the
   a. inner planets.   c. sun.
   b. moon.   d. super nova.
   Answer: C   Difficulty: 1   Section: 1   Objective: 2

5. What bodies in the solar system collided and combined to form Earth?
   a. globules   c. craters
   b. stars   d. planetesimals
   Answer: D   Difficulty: 1   Section: 3   Objective: 1

6. What factors caused the shape and structure of Earth?
   a. gravity and energy   c. gravity and heat
   b. heat and pressure   d. energy and pressure
   Answer: C   Difficulty: 1   Section: 3   Objective: 2

7. Earth's layers formed as rocks melted and
   a. heavier and lighter materials separated.
   b. lava from volcanoes covered Earth.
   c. different landforms developed.
   d. earthquakes caused elements to settle.
   Answer: A   Difficulty: 1   Section: 3   Objective: 1

8. The layer of Earth that extends to the planet's center is the
   a. crust.   c. mantle.
   b. corona.   d. core.
   Answer: D   Difficulty: 1   Section: 3   Objective: 2

9. The middle layer of Earth is the
   a. crust.   c. mantle.
   b. meridian.   d. core.
   Answer: C   Difficulty: 1   Section: 3   Objective: 2

10. The layer of Earth that has the lightest materials is the
    a. mantle.
    b. core.
    c. crust.
    d. ozone.
    Answer: C   Difficulty: 1   Section: 3   Objective: 2

11. Early life-forms released oxygen into Earth's atmosphere through the process of
    a. photosynthesis.
    b. osmosis.
    c. oxidation.
    d. pollination.
    Answer: A   Difficulty: 1   Section: 3   Objective: 3

12. Scientists think that Earth's early atmosphere was made up of
    a. oxygen and water vapor.
    b. carbon dioxide and water vapor.
    c. volcanic gases and dust.
    d. hydrogen and cirrus clouds
    Answer: B   Difficulty: 1   Section: 3   Objective: 3

13. Scientists think oceans may have formed after millions of years of
    a. evaporation
    b. rainfall.
    c. flooding.
    d. humidity.
    Answer: B   Difficulty: 1   Section: 3   Objective: 4

14. Each planet moves around in the sun in
    a. a path the shape of a circle.
    b. a path the shape of an ellipse.
    c. a path the shape of a spiral.
    d. similar-sized orbits.
    Answer: B   Difficulty: 1   Section: 4   Objective: 2

15. The closer a planet is to the sun,
    a. the slower it travels around the sun.
    b. the faster it travels around the sun.
    c. the smaller the angle of its axis.
    d. the greater the angle of its axis.
    Answer: B   Difficulty: 1   Section: 4   Objective: 2

16. The period of a planet's revolution can be used to calculate the planet's
    a. total mass.
    b. total circumference.
    c. distance from the sun.
    d. diameter to the sun.
    Answer: C   Difficulty: 1   Section: 4   Objective: 2

17. The gravitational attraction between two objects increases if
    a. their volumes increase.
    b. their volumes decrease.
    c. the distance between them increases.
    d. the distance between them decreases.
    Answer: D   Difficulty: 1   Section: 4   Objective: 3

18. The gravitational attraction between two objects decreases if
    a. their masses decrease.
    b. their masses increase.
    c. their total area decreases.
    d. their total area increases.
    Answer: A   Difficulty: 1   Section: 4   Objective: 3

19. What is an object's resistance in speed or direction?
    a. gravity
    b. kinetic energy
    c. pressure
    d. inertia
    Answer: D   Difficulty: 1   Section: 4   Objective: 3

20. What caused the solar system to form?
    a. the birth of a nearby star
    b. the collapse of the solar nebula
    c. nuclear fusion in the sun
    d. continuous inertia of the solar
    Answer: B   Difficulty: 1   Section: 1   Objective: 1

21. What two factors affect the gravitational attraction between two objects?
    a. surface area and mass
    b. distance and circumference
    c. volume and mass
    d. distance and mass
    Answer: D   Difficulty: 1   Section: 4   Objective: 3

22. Early organisms added oxygen to Earth's atmosphere as they made food through
    a. photosynthesis.
    b. fission.
    c. germination.
    d. oxidation.
    Answer: A   Difficulty: 1   Section: 3   Objective: 3

23. Earth's period of revolution is about
    a. one day.
    b. one week.
    c. one year.
    d. three months.
    Answer: C   Difficulty: 1   Section: 4   Objective: 1

24. What two opposing forces must stay balanced to keep a nebula from collapsing?
    a. gravity and temperature
    b. inertia and pressure
    c. gravity and pressure
    d. temperature and inertia
    Answer: C   Difficulty: 1   Section: 1   Objective: 1

25. Earth's early continents formed as rocks melted and
    a. absorbed much of the water covering the planet.
    b. lighter materials rose above the ocean's surface.
    c. the heaviest elements rose to form the planet's crust.
    d. sank below the ocean's surface.
    Answer: B   Difficulty: 1   Section: 3   Objective: 4

26. What may have caused oceans to form as Earth's atmosphere changed?
    a. The Earth had cooled enough for heavy rain to fall.
    b. Nitrogen gases condensed into water.
    c. The moon released icy dust particles that crashed into Earth.
    d. Millions of years of meteor showers fell upon Earth.
    Answer: A   Difficulty: 1   Section: 3   Objective: 4

27. The planets of the solar system formed as
    a. the center of the gas cloud cooled.
    b. planetesimals flattened into a rotating disk.
    c. planetesimals collided into one another.
    d. the sun absorbed extra gas and dust from the solar system.
    Answer: C   Difficulty: 1   Section: 1   Objective: 2

28. In what layer of the sun is energy produced?
    a. photosphere
    b. convective zone
    c. chromosphere
    d. core
    Answer: D   Difficulty: 1   Section: 2   Objective: 2

29. What factor allowed the sun to form in the solar system?
    a. the explosion of planetesimals
    b. the division of hydrogen atoms
    c. intense heat at the center of the solar nebula
    d. the division of helium atoms
    Answer: C   Difficulty: 1   Section: 1   Objective: 2

30. How might Earth be affected by the activity of sunspots on the sun's surface?
    a. Sunspot activity might affect Earth's temperatures.
    b. Low sunspot activity might contribute to global warming.
    c. Sunspot activity could send electrically charged particles into Earth's atmosphere.
    d. Sunspot activity has been linked to hurricanes.
    Answer: A   Difficulty: 1   Section: 2   Objective: 3

31. What happens during nuclear fusion in the sun?
    a. Oxygen nuclei combine to form helium.
    b. Helium nuclei combine to form oxygen.
    c. Helium nuclei combine to form hydrogen.
    d. Hydrogen nuclei combine to form helium.
    Answer: D   Difficulty: 1   Section: 2   Objective: 2

32. In a young solar system, new materials are added to planets by
    a. nuclear fusion.   c. the collisions of smaller bodies.
    b. primitive life-forms.   d. convection in planet layers.
    Answer: C   Difficulty: 1   Section: 1   Objective: 2

33. Much of the water of the early oceans may have been
    a. condensed from volcanic gases.
    b. created by the reaction of hydrogen gas and iron.
    c. created by the interaction of UV light and oxygen.
    d. absorbed by Earth's core.
    Answer: A   Difficulty: 1   Section: 3   Objective: 3

34. A planet with a large orbit has a
    a. slow rotation.   c. long period of revolution.
    b. large gas ring.   d. large surface area.
    Answer: C   Difficulty: 1   Section: 4   Objective: 1

35. The dense layer of the sun that blocks light and energy is the
    a. convective zone.   c. photosphere.
    b. radiative zone.   d. chromosphere.
    Answer: B   Difficulty: 1   Section: 2   Objective: 2

36. The gravitational attraction between two objects increases if
    a the distance between them increases and their mass increases.
    b. the distance between them decreases and their mass decreases.
    c. the distance between them increases and their mass decreases.
    d. the distance between them decreases and their mass increases.
    Answer: D   Difficulty: 1   Section: 4   Objective: 3

37. What might sunspots affect on Earth?
    a. electric fields   c. temperatures
    b. magnetic fields   d. plant growth
    Answer: C   Difficulty: 1   Section: 2   Objective: 3

38. What did planetesimals do to form Earth?
    a. collapsed inward   c. left the solar system
    b. orbited the sun   d. crashed and combined
    Answer: D   Difficulty: 1   Section: 3   Objective: 1

39. What caused oceans to form when Earth cooled?
    a. snow   c. steam
    b. rain   d. glaciers
    Answer: B   Difficulty: 1   Section: 3   Objective: 4

40. What happens if objects have more mass and move closer together?
    a. Pressure increases.
    b. Pressure decreases.
    c. Gravity between them increases.
    d. Gravity between them decreases.
    Answer: C   Difficulty: 1   Section: 4   Objective: 3

41. What made the solar system form?
    a. Gravity decreased.
    b. Pressure decreased.
    c. The solar nebula collapsed.
    d. The solar nebula pulled together.
    Answer: C   Difficulty: 1   Section: 1   Objective: 2

42. What happened as light rocks rose to Earth's surface?
    a. Mountains formed.
    b. The oceans got larger.
    c. The mantle got lighter.
    d. Early continents formed.
    Answer: D   Difficulty: 1   Section: 3   Objective: 4

43. How do planets move if they are closer to the sun?
    a. smoother
    b. rougher
    c. slower
    d. faster
    Answer: D   Difficulty: 1   Section: 4   Objective: 2

44. What is used to find a planet's distance from the sun?
    a. the planet's mass
    b. the planet's size
    c. the planet's period of revolution
    d. the planet's number of moons
    Answer: C   Difficulty: 1   Section: 4   Objective: 2

45. What gas was added to the atmosphere change as life-forms carried out photosynthesis?
    a. hydrogen.
    b. oxygen.
    c. sulfur.
    d. argon.
    Answer: B   Difficulty: 1   Section: 3   Objective: 3

46. What process gives the sun its energy?
    a. photosynthesis
    b. cellular regeneration
    c. cellular fission
    d. nuclear fusion
    Answer: D   Difficulty: 1   Section: 2   Objective: 2

47. The famous scientist who made important discoveries about the motion of planets
    around the sun was
    a. Albert Einstein.
    b. Tycho Brache.
    c. Johannes Kepler.
    d. none of the above
    Answer: Johannes Kepler
                      Difficulty: 1   Section: 4   Objective: 2

COMPLETION

Use the terms from the following list to complete the sentences below.

planetesimals	solar flare
orbit	rotation
crust	core
mantle	corona

48. The layer of Earth that extends 2,900 km below the surface and is made of elements such
    as magnesium and iron is the _______________.
    Answer: mantle   Difficulty: 1   Section: 3   Objective: 2

49. If you plant a garden, you use soil from Earth's _______________.
    Answer: crust   Difficulty: 1   Section: 3   Objective: 2

50. Streams of electrically charged particles in space are often emitted from

    _______________.
    Answer: solar flares   Difficulty: 1   Section: 2   Objective: 3

51. The craters that appear on the surface of the moon and other bodies in the solar system probably resulted from collisions with ___________________.

   Answer: planetesimals

   | | Difficulty: 1 | Section: 1 | Objective: 2 |

52. Day and night are caused by the position of Earth during its ___________________.

   Answer: rotation   Difficulty: 1   Section: 4   Objective: 1

53. Earth started to become round as gravity crushed the rock at its ___________________.

   Answer: core   Difficulty: 1   Section: 3   Objective: 1

Use the terms from the following list to complete the sentences below.

solar nebulas	nebulas
globules	orbit
temperature	ellipse
major axis	semimajor axis

54. Earth's orbit has a ___________________ of about 150 million kilometers.

   Answer: semimajor axis

   | | Difficulty: 1 | Section: 4 | Objective: 2 |

55. A star may form after two ___________________ collide.

   Answer: nebulas   Difficulty: 1   Section: 1   Objective: 1

56. The sum of the distances from the edge of the curve to two points inside a(n) ___________________ is always the same.

   Answer: ellipse   Difficulty: 1   Section: 4   Objective: 2

57. The stage is set for stars to form as ___________________ compress and collapse inward.

   Answer: globules   Difficulty: 1   Section: 1   Objective: 1

58. Nuclear fusion occurs in the sun as a result of very high pressure and ___________________.

   Answer: temperatures

   | | Difficulty: 1 | Section: 2 | Objective: 2 |

59. Gravity changes a straight-lined path of a body in space into a curved ___________________.

   Answer: orbit   Difficulty: 1   Section: 4   Objective: 3

Use the terms from the following list to complete the sentences below.

core	nuclear fusion
pressure	period of revolution
rotation	photosphere
sunspots	photosynthesis

60. A giant gas planet has a larger ___________________ than an inner planet.

   Answer: period of revolution

   | | Difficulty: 1 | Section: 4 | Objective: 2 |

61. Activity on the sun's ___________________ can affect Earth's atmosphere.

   Answer: photosphere

   | | Difficulty: 1 | Section: 2 | Objective: 3 |

62. A protective ozone layer in the upper atmosphere eventually formed after millions of years of ___________________ on Earth.

   Answer: photosynthesis

   | | Difficulty: 1 | Section: 3 | Objective: 3 |

63. The tremendous _________________ at the center of the solar nebula was not enough to keep it from collapsing.
    Answer: pressure   Difficulty: 1   Section: 1   Objective: 1

64. The formula $E = mc^2$ shows how small amounts of matter can produce energy during the process of _________________.
    Answer: nuclear fusion
                          Difficulty: 1   Section: 2   Objective: 2

65. When magnetic fields slow down the activity in the convective zone, _________________ form on the sun's surface.
    Answer: sunspots   Difficulty: 1   Section: 2   Objective: 2

Use the terms from the following list to complete the sentences below.

rotation	solar nebula
major axis	law of universal gravitation
crust	radiative zone
revolution	convective zone

66. Mercury completes a _________________ around the sun in less time than the other eight planets in the solar system.
    Answer: revolution   Difficulty: 1   Section: 4   Objective: 1

67. Sir Isaac Newton used the _________________ to explain why planets closest to the sun move faster.
    Answer: law of universal gravitation
                          Difficulty: 1   Section: 4   Objective: 3

68. The densest region of the sun that disperses energy in different directions is called the _________________.
    Answer: radiative zone
                          Difficulty: 1   Section: 2   Objective: 2

69. Half of the _________________ of a planet's orbit describes the planet's maximum distance to the sun.
    Answer: major axis   Difficulty: 1   Section: 4   Objective: 2

70. As gas clouds collapse and temperature increases, a _________________ may form.
    Answer: solar nebula
                          Difficulty: 1   Section: 1   Objective: 1

71. Thermal energy moves from the sun's interior by the circulation of gases in the _________________.
    Answer: convective zone
                          Difficulty: 1   Section: 2   Objective: 2

Use the terms from the following list to complete the sentences below.

sunspot	mantle
fusion	solar flare
crust	globule
revolution	rotation
nebula	

72. The layer of Earth that has low-density materials is the _________________.
    Answer: crust   Difficulty: 1   Section: 3   Objective: 2

73. A large, interstellar cloud of gas and dust is called a _________________.
    Answer: nebula   Difficulty: 1   Section: 1   Objective: 1

74. The sun is powered by nuclear _______________.
    Answer: fusion   Difficulty: 1   Section: 2   Objective: 2

75. A cooler area of the photosphere that may affect climate on Earth is a

    _______________.
    Answer: sunspot   Difficulty: 1   Section: 2   Objective: 3

76. Earth completes one _______________ each day.
    Answer: rotation   Difficulty: 1   Section: 4   Objective: 1

Use the terms from the following list to complete the sentences below.

    solar nebula   pressure
    photosphere   convective
    zone

77. Gravity and _______________ must balance each other to hold a nebula together.
    Answer: pressure   Difficulty: 1   Section: 1   Objective: 1

78. The solar system was formed from a cloud called the _______________.
    Answer: solar nebula
                      Difficulty: 1   Section: 1   Objective: 2

79. Gases circulate and carry energy to the sun's surface from the _______________.
    Answer: convection zone
                      Difficulty: 1   Section: 2   Objective: 2

80. Energy leaves the sun from the layer we see called the _______________.
    Answer: photosphere
                      Difficulty: 1   Section: 2   Objective: 2

SHORT ANSWER

81. Briefly state Kepler's three laws of planetary motion.
    Answer:
        Answers will vary. Sample answer: Kepler's first law of motion states that all planets
        move around the sun in elliptical orbits. Kepler's second law states that planets move
        faster when they are closer to the sun. Kepler's third law states that if a planet's period
        of revolution is known, the planet's distance from the sun can be calculated.
    Difficulty: 2   Section: 4   Objective: 2

82. How did the interior of Earth separate into layers?
    Answer:
        Answers will vary. Sample answer: When the inside of early Earth had melted, gravity
        caused the heavier elements, like nickel and iron, to sink to the center. Lighter
        elements floated to the surface. Over time, this process cause Earth to separate into
        layers.
    Difficulty: 2   Section: 3   Objective: 2

83. How do gravity and pressure keep a nebula from collapsing?
    Answer:
        Answers will vary. Sample answer: As particles in a nebula collide and move away
        from each other, pressure is created. The outward pressure balances the inward
        gravitational pull, and the nebula becomes stable.
    Difficulty: 2   Section: 1   Objective: 1

84. How do planets form?
    Answer:
        Particles swirling in a cloud of dust and gas stick together, forming planetestimals,
        which accumulate more matter and finally form planets.
    Difficulty: 2   Section: 1   Objective: 2

85. How do you know that gravity does not produce the sun's energy?
    Answer:
       If all of the sun's gravitational energy were released, the sun would last only
       45 million years. The solar system is at least 4.6 billion years old.
    Difficulty: 2   Section: 2   Objective: 2

86. How does energy produced by nuclear fusion move from the sun's core to space?
    Answer:
       It moves very slowly through the radiative zone, circulates through the convective
       zone, and passes through the photosphere and into the chromosphere and corona.
    Difficulty: 2   Section: 2   Objective: 2

87. How and when did oxygen become abundant in Earth's atmosphere?
    Answer:
       Some time before 3.4 million years ago, life-forms evolved that produced oxygen as a
       byproduct of photosynthesis; over millions of years, oxygen levels increased.
    Difficulty: 2   Section: 3   Objective: 3

88. How has the relationship between ozone and life on Earth changed since the time of
    Earth's early atmosphere?
    Answer:
       The absence of ozone in Earth 's early atmosphere allowed molecules to be broken
       apart by UV radiation. These broken-down molecules combined to form the complex
       molecules that gave rise to life. Currently, the ozone layer protects life on Earth from
       the harmful effects of UV radiation.
    Difficulty: 3   Section: 3   Objective: 3

MATCHING

a. nebula   d. pressure
b. solar nebula   e. gravity
c. temperature   f. planetesimals

89. ___ the force that holds together the matter of a nebula
    Answer: E   Difficulty: 1   Section: 1   Objective: 1
90. ___ the force created as particles in a nebula push away from each other
    Answer: D   Difficulty: 1   Section: 1   Objective: 1
91. ___ large bodies that became the cores of current planets
    Answer: F   Difficulty: 1   Section: 1   Objective: 2
92. ___ the cloud of gas and dust that formed our solar system
    Answer: B   Difficulty: 1   Section: 1   Objective: 2
93. ___ a large cloud of gas and dust in interstellar space
    Answer: A   Difficulty: 1   Section: 1   Objective: 2
94. ___ a measure of the energy of motion of the particles in an object
    Answer: C   Difficulty: 1   Section: 1   Objective: 2

a. nuclear fusion   f. radiative zone
b. sunspots   g. convective zone
c. solar flares   h. photosphere
d. core   i. climate
e. corona   j. magnetic fields

95. ___ giant eruptions on the sun's surface
    Answer: C   Difficulty: 1   Section: 2   Objective: 3
96. ___ caused by the rotation and movement of energy of the sun, and reach far out into
    space
    Answer: J   Difficulty: 1   Section: 2   Objective: 3

97. ____ the visible surface of the sun
    Answer: H   Difficulty: 1   Section: 2   Objective: 1
98. ____ a dense layer of the sun where light and energy are blocked and sent into different directions
    Answer: F   Difficulty: 1   Section: 2   Objective: 2

99. ____ when two or more nuclei fuse to form another nucleus; the source of the sun's energy
    Answer: A   Difficulty: 1   Section: 2   Objective: 2
100. ____ may be affected on Earth by the surface activity of the sun
    Answer: I   Difficulty: 1   Section: 2   Objective: 3
101. ____ cooler, dark areas of the photosphere of the sun
    Answer: B   Difficulty: 1   Section: 2   Objective: 3
102. ____ the layer of the sun where gases circulate and carry energy to the visible surface of the sun
    Answer: G   Difficulty: 1   Section: 2   Objective: 2
103. ____ the outermost layer of the sun
    Answer: E   Difficulty: 1   Section: 2   Objective: 1
104. ____ where the suns' energy is made; the innermost layer of the sun
    Answer: D   Difficulty: 1   Section: 2   Objective: 1

a. rotation   c. revolution
b. orbit   d. period of revolution

105. ____ one complete trip along an orbit
    Answer: C   Difficulty: 1   Section: 4   Objective: 1
106. ____ the path of a body that travels around another body in space
    Answer: B   Difficulty: 1   Section: 4   Objective: 1
107. ____ the amount of time it takes a body to complete a trip along an orbit
    Answer: D   Difficulty: 1   Section: 4   Objective: 1
108. ____ the spin of a body on its axis
    Answer: A   Difficulty: 1   Section: 4   Objective: 1

a. sunspot   f. nebula
b. revolution   g. nuclear fusion
c. rotation   h. crust
d. orbit   i. photosphere
e. mantle   j. solar flare

109. ____ the visible layer of the sun
    Answer: I   Difficulty: 1   Section: 2   Objective: 2

110. ____ a complete trip along an orbit
    Answer: B   Difficulty: 1   Section: 4   Objective: 1
111. ____ the process that provides the sun with its energy
    Answer: G   Difficulty: 1   Section: 2   Objective: 2
112. ____ the layer of Earth that formed as lighter materials floated to the surface
    Answer: H   Difficulty: 1   Section: 3   Objective: 1
113. ____ the spinning of a body on its axis
    Answer: C   Difficulty: 1   Section: 4   Objective: 1
114. ____ the layer of Earth above the core
    Answer: E   Difficulty: 1   Section: 3   Objective: 1
115. ____ a huge eruption on the surface of the sun
    Answer: J   Difficulty: 1   Section: 2   Objective: 3
116. ____ a cooler, dark area of the photosphere that has a strong magnetic field
    Answer: A   Difficulty: 1   Section: 2   Objective: 3

117. ___ the path a body follows as it travels around another body in space
    Answer: D   Difficulty: 1   Section: 4   Objective: 1

118. ___ a cloud of gas and dust from which bodies in space are formed
    Answer: F   Difficulty: 1   Section: 1   Objective: 2

    a. crust   c. core
    b. mantle

119. ___ Earth's central layer
    Answer: C   Difficulty: 1   Section: 3   Objective: 2

120. ___ the outer layer of Earth
    Answer: A   Difficulty: 1   Section: 3   Objective: 2

121. ___ the middle layer of Earth
    Answer: B   Difficulty: 1   Section: 3   Objective: 2

    a. ellipse   b. orbit
    c. rotation   d. revolution

122. ___ the spin of a planet on its axis
    Answer: C   Difficulty: 1   Section: 4   Objective: 1

123. ___ one complete trip around the sun
    Answer: D   Difficulty: 1   Section: 4   Objective: 1

124. ___ the path a planet follows when it travels around the sun
    Answer: B   Difficulty: 1   Section: 4   Objective: 1

125. ___ shape of the path a planet follows when it travels around the sun
    Answer: A   Difficulty: 1   Section: 4   Objective: 1

ESSAY

126. Why do the planets of the solar system have different qualities even though they came from the same nebula?
Answer:
Answers will vary. Sample answer: Planets were affected by their distance to the sun as they formed. For example, planetesimals that formed near the outside of the solar nebula attracted nebula gases. As a result, they're abundant in hydrogen and helium. Planets that formed near the center of the nebula were too hot to attract gases, so they are mostly made of rock.
Difficulty: 3   Section: 1   Objective: 1

127. Why are the planets in the solar system shaped like spheres?
Answer:
Answers will vary. Sample answer: Planets are shaped like spheres because gravity pulls all of their material toward the center with equal force. In a sphere, each point on the surface is the same distance from the center.
Difficulty: 2   Section: 1   Objective: 1

128. How might Earth's atmosphere be affected if large areas of forest are cut down for human construction?
Answer:
Answers will vary. Sample answer: If human construction replaced large areas of land that were abundant in plant growth, there might not be as much oxygen in the atmosphere. The amount of carbon dioxide in the atmosphere might also increase.
Difficulty: 2   Section: 3   Objective: 2

129. Have students explain how energy released from the collision of two protons in the sun's core warms a car seat on Earth. Students should account for the following: nuclear fusion, the movement of energy through the radiative and convective zones, Earth 's atmosphere, and the amount of time this process takes.

Answer:

The collision of the two protons (hydrogen) would result in a larger single nucleus (of helium). This nuclear fusion would release a very large amount of energy. This energy is produced in the sun's core. From the core, energy is sent from the radiative zone to the convective zone. The gases circulate in the convective zone. The hot gases carry energy to the photosphere, or the visible surface of the sun. Energy leaves the photosphere and reaches the car seat on Earth in 8.3 minutes.

Difficulty: 3   Section: 2   Objective: 2

INTERPRETING GRAPHICS

Use the image below to answer the following questions.

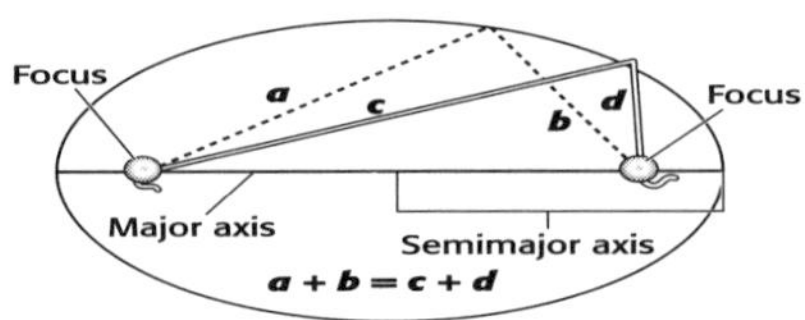

130. ___ The shape of the ellipse above describes
   a. the cross section of the sun.
   b. the shape of a planet's core.
   c. the path of a planet's axis.
   d. a planet's orbit around the sun.
   Answer: D   Difficulty: 1   Section: 4   Objective: 2

131. ___ The length of the semimajor axis can be used to describe
   a. the surface area of the sun.
   b. the radius of the sun.
   c. the distance between a planet and the sun.
   d. the radius of a planet's orbit around the sun.
   Answer: C   Difficulty: 1   Section: 4   Objective: 2

132. ___ The longer the length of the semimajor axis,
   a. the longer it takes a planet to orbit the sun.
   b. the longer it takes energy to leave the sun.
   c. the faster a planet can spin on its axis.
   d. the heavier the mass of a planet.
   Answer: A   Difficulty: 1   Section: 4   Objective: 2

Use the graph below to answer question 17.

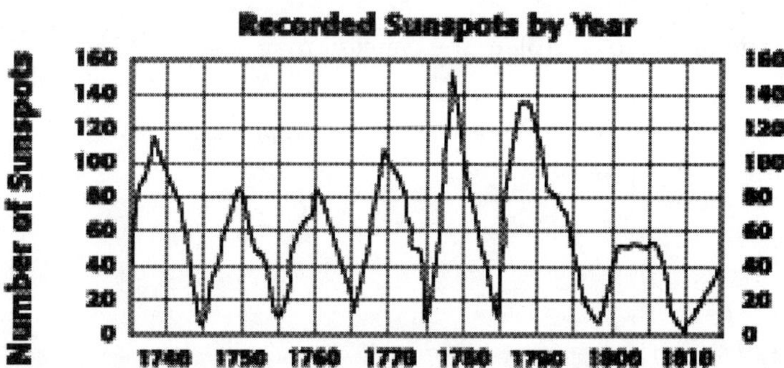

133. The graph shows the number of sunspots recorded each year from 1735 to 1815. About how much time passed between the year with the most sunspots and the year with the fewest sunspots? Explain your answer.

Answer:

Answers will vary. Sample answer: The most sunspots were recorded around the year 1778, and the fewest were recorded in the year 1810. About 32 years passed between the years of highest and lowest sunspot activity.

Difficulty: 1   Section: 2   Objective: 3

CONCEPT MAPPING

134. Use the following terms to complete the concept map below:

<table>
<tr><td>planetesimals</td><td>gas</td></tr>
<tr><td>nebula</td><td>planets</td></tr>
<tr><td>solar system</td><td>gravity</td></tr>
<tr><td>solar nebula</td><td>rock</td></tr>
</table>

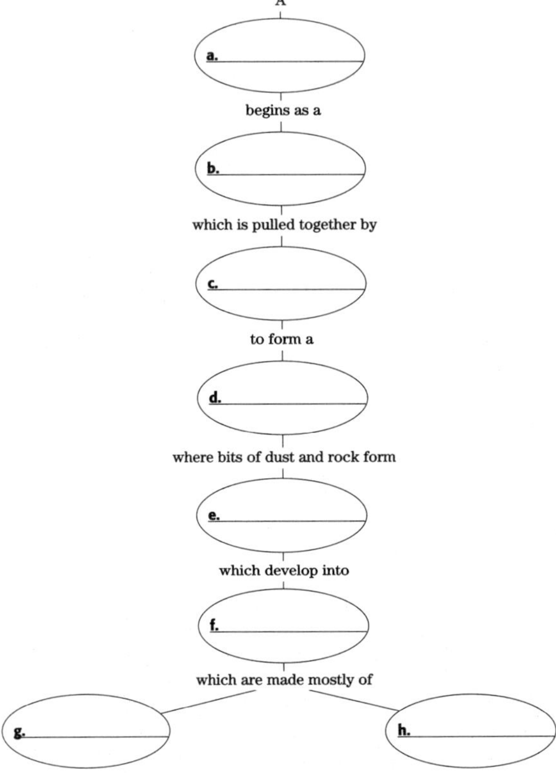

Answer:
  a. solar system; b. nebula; c. gravity; d. solar nebula; e. planetesimals;
  f. planets; rock, gas.

Difficulty: 3   Section: 1   Objective: 2